Bullfinches, Chaffinches & Bramblings

Peter Lander and Bob Partridge
Photographs by Dennis Avon MIOP ARPS

(Popular British Birds in Aviculture series: No 4)

Bullfinches, Chaffinches & Bramblings

Bullfinches, Chaffinches & Bramblings

Peter Lander and Bob Partridge

© 1998 Kingdom Books England. All rights reserved. No part of this publication may be reproduced, stored in a retrieval system, or transmitted in any form or by any means, electronic, mechanical, photocopying, recording or otherwise, without the written permission of the publisher.

Published by Kingdom Books
PO Box 15
Waterlooville PO7 6BQ
England

Bullfinches, Chaffinches & Bramblings

Contents

PREFACE	5
CHAPTER 1: Cages and Aviaries	6
CHAPTER 2: Evolution	12
CHAPTER 3: Lifestyle in the Wild – Bullfinches	14
CHAPTER 4: Accommodation and Foods – Bullfinches	20
CHAPTER 5: Breeding – Bullfinches	25
CHAPTER 6: Lifestyle in the Wild – Chaffinches	29
CHAPTER 7: Lifestyle in the Wild – Bramblings	33
CHAPTER 8: Accommodation and Foods – Chaffinches and Bramblings	37
CHAPTER 9: Breeding – Chaffinches and Bramblings	40
CHAPTER 10: Ringing	44
CHAPTER 11: Exhibition	47
CHAPTER 12: Mules and Hybrids	53
CHAPTER 13: Mutations and Colour Variants	57
CHAPTER 14: The Law	63
TRIBUTE	64

Preface

This book is the fourth in a series intended as a follow-on to the very successful book British Birds in Aviculture, published in conjunction with the British Bird Council. By concentrating on no more than three species in each book we can treat them in much greater depth. It also enables us to update the original book where necessary in the light of the latest knowledge and experience.

Our old friend the late Walter Lewis always used to say, 'The golden rule in bird breeding is that there is no golden rule.' By this he meant that there are always exceptions in anything to do with birds, and the experience of one successful breeder is totally different to that of another, for no apparent reason. Walter was considered to be one of the most knowledgeable British fanciers of his time in the field of British birds, mules and hybrids.

All we can do is pass on our knowledge and experience as a basis on which each breeder can develop his or her own system. As joint authors we can sometimes give different information, hopefully making this book all the more interesting and useful.

Peter Lander and Bob Partridge

Popular British Birds in Aviculture series:

No 1: Greenfinches   *No 2: Siskins and Goldfinches*

No 3: Redpolls, Twites and Linnets   *No 4: Bullfinches, Chaffinches and Bramblings*

Chapter 1

Cages and Aviaries

Before obtaining any birds it is essential to have suitable accommodation. While this need be neither expensive nor ornamental, it must be suitable for the birds' needs. They must have room to move about freely, shelter from the elements and protection from enemies such as cats, owls, weasels, rats and other vermin. There must also be sufficient receptacles to provide the necessary food and water.

Birds certainly look better in an aviary but, for those who have neither the space nor the means, adequate accommodation can be provided in cages. These can be situated in a shed in the garden. However, many sheds need extra windows to allow the birds enough light to feed throughout the day - if the shed is dark they will spend a lot of time roosting. There must be good ventilation allowing continuous free passage of air. Heating is not necessary for temperate-zone birds normally resident in this country throughout the year. On the other hand, it is essential that the birds can drink at all times during the day and, unless the fancier is at home all day, the shed should be heated or insulated sufficiently to prevent the water from freezing during severe weather. A study of the advertisements in the fancy press will produce information on sheds in a variety of shapes and sizes, all designed for bird keeping.

Birds need room if they are to breed - in fact the larger the cage the better. The minimum size recommended is 91cm (36in) wide by 60cm (24in) high by 46cm (18in) back to front containing only one pair. Far better results will be obtained by having a few pairs in large cages than by having more pairs in smaller cages. Natural branches can be fixed in the cages for perches; these look nicer and are much more comfortable for the birds' feet than the round doweling often used, but do not overcrowd the cage with these as flying space is essential. In one end of the cage fix a bunch of conifer or other suitable evergreen, with a forked branch in the middle to support a nest. Alternatively a small wicker basket or half-open-fronted, open-topped box can be used (fig 1). The object is to provide privacy and a feeling of security to the sitting hen, but the bunch must not be thick enough to exclude too much light or prevent the birds from entering easily: just enough to give the necessary seclusion.

Contrary to advice frequently given, the most consistent results are obtained in sheds and aviaries facing east. This is because birds, particularly when nesting, do not like being

Cages and Aviaries

subjected to the mid-day sun and, in the wild, nearly always choose a shaded position. They also like protection from the prevailing west winds and, in the wild, choose a situation that is protected in this respect also. It is not always possible to provide the ideal so it is advisable to fix up some means of providing shade and protection.

The only real disadvantage to cage breeding is the extra work involved in providing a sufficient variety of foods on which the birds can feed their young, particularly when they are first hatched. Even in a small aviary it is much easier to provide a variety of foods, and the birds will find a few insects to supplement their diet, which can be so beneficial in the early stages of a chick's life. To some extent this can be overcome if the birds can be persuaded to feed the young ones on egg food. More details are given in chapters 4 and 8.

Fig 1: Nest box

It is not essential to provide near natural conditions to breed our popular native birds. The majority of these common species can be reproduced with the minimum of cover in a small flight. Even a large cage will suffice for many of the hardbills.

Mozambique siskin x bullfinch hybrid

Chapter 1

Some years ago breeders used large amounts of cover in the form of gorse, broom, conifers and other evergreens but nowadays the birds are much more domesticated and breed very successfully with only a minimum of cover. This has the added benefit of allowing the breeder to observe, study and enjoy the birds to a far greater degree.

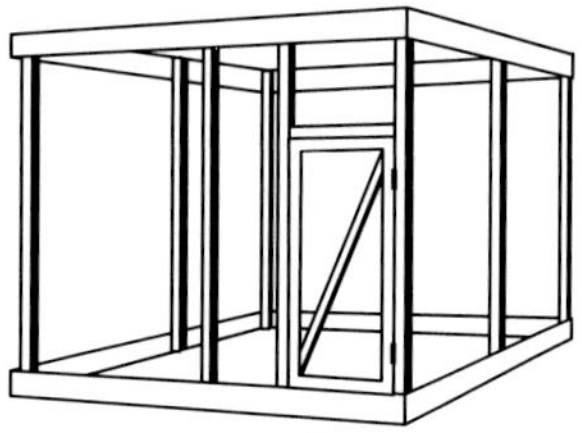

Aviary Construction

Fig 2: Typical Aviary – from an original design by Hylton Blythe

An aviary can be any size but the minimum recommended is 180cm (6ft) long by 60cm (2ft) wide by 180cm (6ft) high. This will hold approximately six non-breeding birds, but generally only one pair of breeding birds. In a mixed aviary one should allow at least 2.25 cubic metres (80 cubic feet) per pair of birds; much more if possible.

Aviaries can be as simple or as elaborate as one wishes, depending on circumstances and funds available, as long as they meet the requirements of the birds. An example of a cheap and easily-constructed aviary is the one designed some years ago by Mr Hylton Blythe (fig 2), which is made as follows. Roofing laths are driven into the ground at 1m (3ft) intervals and cut off to the required height, with further laths nailed along the top and across from side to side. This enables 1m (3ft) wire netting to be stapled to the laths. There is a small door at one end for access, with a shelf above it for food. A further small door gives access to the shelf so that it is not necessary to enter the aviary to feed the birds. Cover must be provided to keep the seed and shelf dry. The birds also need protection from the wind and rain and shade from the sun. This can be achieved by nailing boards all round along the top to a width of about 30cm (12in) and the same along the top of the sides. Roofing felt can be used instead of boards if there is wire netting underneath to support it. If all the timber is treated with creosote or bitumen it will last much longer.

Where funds allow, more substantial aviaries give added protection to the birds and last considerably longer. A well-constructed and well-maintained aviary can more than repay the extra expense and labour. For example, solid foundation plinths set well into the ground constructed of 10cm (4in) bricks, blocks or solid concrete 45cm (14in) deep will keep out rats. The base area can then be filled in with earth, pebbles, sand, bark chippings or solid concrete or slabs for easy cleaning and disinfecting. Tanalised framing or cedar wood 5cm x 5cm (2in x 2in) will last almost a life time.

Solid timber felted roofs give valuable protection from cats, kestrels, marauding magpies and thunderstorms and also exclude droppings from wild birds, which can pass on disease to the aviary inmates. Solid cladding of the back and at least one third of the sides gives added protection as well as security to the birds (fig 3).

Large feeding trays can be provided in a completely dry area where they are clear of any perches, thus preventing the birds from eating mouldy or soiled foods. These and many other refinements can all be considered for the welfare of the birds, which is paramount if success is to be achieved.

For nesting sites, use small wickerwork baskets with a few twigs tacked around. This gives the birds some degree of privacy. Even so, many birds pick nesting sites completely open to view, despite other more secluded sites being available. Two or three sites should be available to each pair of birds. Provide a little extra cover for any particularly shy specimens. Other acceptable nesting sites are square wooden pans with perforated zinc bottoms. These are used by many breeders of canaries. Canary plastic pans will need to have felt linings glued or sewn inside, but the birds often pull these to pieces, leaving the slippery plastic surface on which they cannot shape a nest. However, a little polyfilla or plaster of Paris wiped roughly around the inside can be helpful. Plywood or cane strawberry punnets or clay flower pots can also be utilised. Sites and receptacles used will depend on what the birds find acceptable.

Any simple structure with suitably-sized netting will keep birds in, but it is much more difficult to keep

Cages and Aviaries

vermin out. Some refinements have already been mentioned to overcome this but, if you do not intend to have solid plinths and solid roofs, other methods have to be used. Cats can be a nuisance, especially if they get on the top of an aviary. To overcome this the main frame should be extended about 23cm (9in) and this extension covered with 5cm (2in) netting, often called chicken wire. Cats have difficulty in walking on this netting, and bunches of gorse hung facing downwards on the corner posts will help to stop them climbing up.

Rats, if they gain access, will kill the birds and drag them down their holes, so that they all suddenly disappear. This can be overcome by digging a trench round the aviary 30cm (12in) deep and 30cm (12in) wide. The wire netting is extended down the side of the trench and along the bottom in the shape of a letter L. The trench is then filled in.

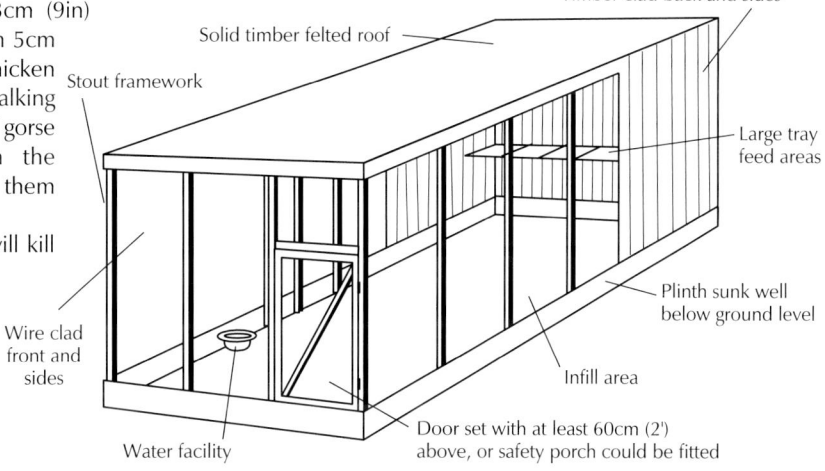

Fig 3: A well constructed aviary 1.8m x 3.6m x 1.8m (6ft x 12ft x 6ft) would accommodate 4 mixed pairs or up to 20 non-breeding birds

Mice are much more difficult to exclude. Although they do not kill birds directly, they carry diseases and cause considerable disturbance, jeopardising breeding results. Also, where mice can get in, weasels will follow and they kill and eat every bird in sight in no time at all. Mice and weasels can get through 1.3cm (0.5in) netting which is generally used for aviaries: 1cm (0.4in) netting, which is much more expensive, will keep out all but baby mice. It is therefore very important to keep a sharp look out, and take quick action if any signs of mice are seen by setting traps and putting down poison. Both traps and poison must be suitably protected from pets and children, especially as they generally cannot be placed inside the aviary. There are now, however, some traps which catch the mice alive and which can be used inside an aviary safely.

A small aviary for each pair of birds is considered ideal, especially if it is your intention to specialise in a particular species. On the other hand, large aviaries containing several species, such as pairs of redpolls, siskins, linnets, twites and goldfinches, will prove perfectly satisfactory. Greenfinches can usually be trusted with these smaller finches throughout the year, and can also be housed with finches of their own size, such as bullfinches, chaffinches, bramblings or buntings, outside the breeding season, though it is not recommended that these species are mixed during the breeding season. Housing of all species needs careful consideration to suit individual needs.

Trouble can be experienced when just two pairs of different species are kept and

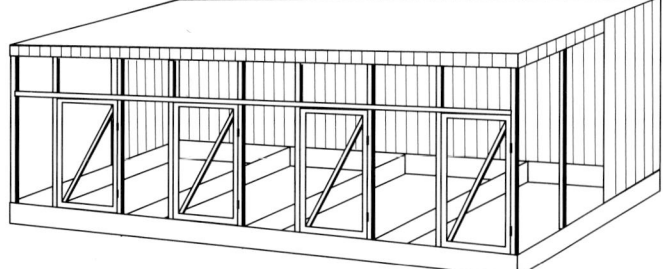

Fig 4: A similar sized aviary partitioned to take 4 segregated breeding pairs; a front corridor could be added for safety

9

Chapter 1

Isolated Type of Nesting Site

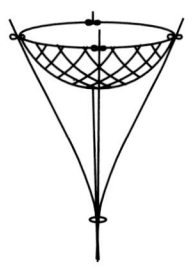

a: Basket wired to stout twigs

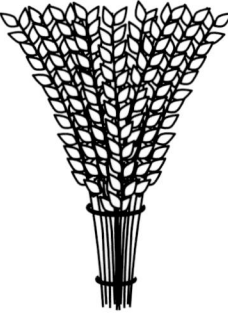

b: Surrounded by evergreen twigs and wire-tied

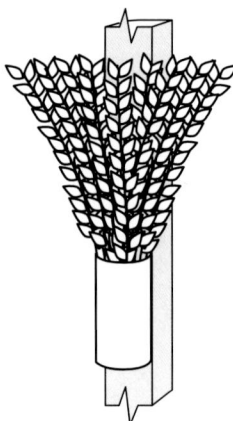

c: Finished nesting site inserted in down-pipe which has been fixed to framework

Fig 5: Nesting sites

bred in one aviary, because one pair will sometimes chase the other continually, preventing feeding. It is best to have either one pair or three or more pairs in a flight. This usually prevents the trouble, but always provide a large feeding area or several smaller ones.

The pros and cons of different materials for the floor area, touched on earlier, are really governed by the conditions and needs of both the birds and the keeper. Earth is the natural floor covering and, provided that overstocking is avoided, the birds can derive much benefit in the form of trace elements from the soil. Waste seeds which germinate are a welcome addition to the birds' diet. The vegetation attracts a myriad of insect life, which again is very beneficial, especially when young are being reared. The drawback is that it is difficult to prevent mice from burrowing in and breeding in the aviary, contaminating both the food and the soil. Earth floors are also difficult to disinfect and keep clean. Liming annually will help to keep it sweet, but the soil will undoubtedly need renewing completely to a depth of 15cm (6in) every few years if problems with disease are to be avoided. Small washed pebbles, laid to a depth of 10-15cm (4-6in), are a good alternative. Seeds will still germinate and the birds derive benefit from searching amongst the pebbles. Mice will not take up residence if a good depth of loose pebbles is maintained. Pebbles can easily be riddled to remove waste, washed and disinfected.

Forest bark chippings on an earth floor can look very attractive and again discourage mice if a good covering is maintained. The bark should be about 8-10cm (3-4in) deep and will need to be raked over now and again to freshen it up. It will also need to be removed and replenished from time to time. The spent bark can be composted and used in the garden.

Concrete is sterile and stark and can be cold and damp during inclement weather, but the dampness can be almost eliminated by laying plastic sheeting down before concreting. A layer of sand on top of the finished floor will take away the starkness. It has the advantage of being easy to clean and disinfect and is rodent-proof.

Solid wood floors are also worth considering, having similar benefits to concrete, but being much warmer. However, this type of floor will need to be raised some 30cm (12in) above the ground, allowing a good air flow beneath it to prevent rotting and stopping rodents from gaining access. The whole structure can be set on stilts such as concrete pillars or blocks and bricks with plenty of ventilation holes.

We now come to furnishing the aviary. Most hardbills, especially bullfinches, quickly defoliate any living plants and shrubs. Most will not survive such treatment for long, although vegetation such as elderberry, blackberry and stinging nettles sometimes survives if the aviary is not over-populated. The aviary should be furnished with natural branches such as willow, ash, elder, hazel, apple or pear. These should be located sparsely and high up, providing safe perching and roosting places but still leaving plenty of space for flying exercise.

Since growing shrubs are not usually practical when you are keeping hardbills, substitutes must be provided. There are various ways of doing this using evergreen branches from the conifer tree family. Where single pairs are housed a couple of isolated nesting sites will be found adequate. These are made by wiring a few short branches or twigs of the chosen evergreen around a wickerwork basket or some other similar receptacle (fig 5). For most birds these should be fixed fairly high, close to the roof. Short lengths of gutter down pipe (approximately 15cm (6in) of 6.5cm (2.5in) diameter) screwed to the framework in suitable places as nesting sites can easily be fixed and replaced as required. Where several pairs are housed together at least two such sites must be provided for each pair. They can also be made a little more substantial to give each pair more privacy. This will help avoid the odd skirmish of pairs guarding territory.

Many breeders find the hedge system by far the most satisfactory. Strange to say, a continuous hedge all down one side or the back seems to overcome territorial problems, and pairs nest close to each other without any fighting. The artificial hedge is built in the following way. Vertical spacers about 5cm (2in) thick are fastened to the side of the aviary. Then laths are nailed horizontally about 25cm (10in) apart, starting from the top. It is not necessary to go below about 75cm (30in) from the floor. If possible, choose the west or south-west side. If the outside of this part of the aviary is of wood, or some other solid material, so much the better. If not, cover it with hessian or roofing felt to provide protection and privacy. Bare, forked branches are now placed in the laths to simulate the inside of a hedge.

After this, conifer branches or other evergreens such as heather and gorse are threaded into the laths, producing a finish rather like an uncut hedge. It is important that this is not too thick and that there are holes in the foliage through which the birds can obtain access to the inside of the hedge where they will build their nests. Do not forget to put a covering 30-46cm (12-18in) wide on the outside of the aviary over the top of the hedge to provide shade from the sun and shelter from the rain.

If birds are to be kept in a very open-type aviary all the year round, it is best to attach some sort of shelter shed to it so that the feeding can be done inside, and it may be necessary on occasions to confine the birds inside as well. The shelter shed can be as large or small as you desire, or it can be the main bird room with the aviary built on the side. A container full of grit and a bath of fresh water are other essentials to the aviary.

If the birds are being bred in cages in a shed it is very helpful to have a small flight built on to the end of the shed. The birds are fed inside the shed with a pop-hole to give access to the flight. Young birds, when fully weaned, can be transferred to this flight, leaving the parents free to get on with the next nest. Most birds moult out better in a flight where they have access to fresh air with plenty of exercise and bathing facilities.

It is recommended that all birds be ringed, and it is worth bearing this point in mind when deciding on the feeding stations. For some pairs it is a great help if the feeding stations can be somewhat obscured from the nesting sites.

As previously mentioned, aviaries can be as large or small, as ornamental or heavily-built, as the owner wishes, but all will follow the basic pattern of design described and illustrated in the sketches. Refinements can be added according to individual taste.

One point that should be stressed is that it is better not to have the doors too large unless a safety porch is included. If doors are made 90cm-120cm (3-4ft) high and approximately 60cm (2ft) wide an area of 60-90cm (2-3ft) will be left above the door on the usual 2m (6ft) aviary. Birds flying towards the door will go to this space above it as you approach and enter, reducing the possibility of escape. The door should be set well clear of the ground so as not to impede its opening and closing on entry or exit. Doors can open inwards or outwards to suit the needs of the keeper.

Rambler roses, honeysuckle, clematis, hop and other climbing plants can be grown up the outside of the aviary. They look very attractive and help to attract greenfly and other insects from which the birds will benefit. However, care needs to be taken that the growth does not interfere with the general maintenance of the aviary. If the growth penetrates the wire netting for a prolonged period it can soon create holes that are large enough for birds to escape. This can easily happen before the damage is noticed by the keeper.

Chapter 2

Evolution

There is a considerable gap in evolutionary terms between the *Carduelis* finches such as the greenfinch, the goldfinch or the redpoll, and the *Pyrrhula* group known as bullfinches. The genus *Pyrrhula* consists of a small group of six or eight species and some 15 to 17 races are recognised within the group (depending on the authority concerned). The species are *Pyrrhula pyrrhula*, *P aurantiala*, *P erythal*, *P erythrocephala*, *P leucogenys* and *P nipalensis*. Apart from *P leucogenys*, which is confined to the Philippines, they all range through Europe, extending eastward and northward through Asia. All have adapted to feeding mainly on tree seeds and buds. Their closest relatives appear to be the trumpeter and desert finches of the small genus *Rhodopechys* which appear closely allied to the much larger and more widespread genus of *Carpodacus* (the Rose finches). The Grosbeaks and their close cousin the Hawfinch *(Coccothraustes)* may also be closely related to the *Pyrrhula* group, as they have similar feeding habits and cheek pouches (see chapter 3) for storing food rather than the larger storage crops of the Carduelis finches. *Pyrrhula pyrrhula* can be divided into about 10 recognised races. With one exception, those situated in the Western regions of Europe are the most brightly coloured: the males have more pink or red and the females are a richer brownish hue, while the races from the eastern regions are predominantly grey.

In evolutionary terms there appears to be a gap between the Pyrrhula and Fringilla group. The Fringilla group consists of the following three species:
- the chaffinch *(Fringilla coelebs)*, which includes our British and European races.
- the brambling *(Fringilla montifringilla)*, which is a very closely related, northerly breeding form of chaffinch.
- the larger blue chaffinch *(Fringilla teypea)* of the Canary Islands.

All are territorial and highly insectivorous during the breeding season but form foraging flocks at other times.

According to the scientists there is a difference between the British chaffinch *(Fringilla coelebs gengleri)* and the European chaffinch *(F c coelebs)*, although they look alike. The European chaffinch is generally a little darker in body colour, and it migrates in the winter, while the British one does not. In winter British chaffinches gather together locally

12

Evolution

into small flocks of about a dozen cocks and hens. European chaffinches gather into large flocks to migrate. Some predominantly male flocks winter in Britain (hence the chaffinch's country name of 'bachelor finch') and some predominantly female flocks winter as far west as Ireland. Another interesting thing about the chaffinch is that its song varies in different parts of the country. Although essentially the same song, it has been found there are quite distinct local dialects!

The more easterly races of the *Fringilla coelebs*, including the *africana*, have much paler body colouration and are unlikely to be confused with *F c gengleri* or *F c coelebs*. These eastern races inhabit North Africa and Turkey in the main as well as parts of the Middle East. There are records of some of these races interbreeding where their ranges meet, but not with the European chaffinch, numbers of which winter in North Africa.

The brambling *(Fringilla montifringilla)* breeds close to and all along the Arctic Circle. It is forced to vacate this area in the winter, migrating south right down to the Mediterranean as well as Asia.

Northern bullfinch hen

Some come across to the British Isles and Ireland when food supplies are low in Southern Europe. Very large influxes have been recorded in some years.

There are no close relatives or similar birds to the chaffinches and brambling in either South Africa (except for introduced species) or South America, so we must assume that these species evolved long after their ancestors left the south and are relatively new in evolutionary terms.

Chapter 3

Lifestyle in the Wild -
Bullfinches

Order: Passeriformes
Family: Fringillidae (Finches)
Genus: *Pyrrhula*
Species: *Pyrrhula pyrrhula pileata*
Common Name: Bullfinch

Description
Length: 15.25cm (6in)
Weight: approximately 26g (1oz)
Wing Span: 20.25cm (8in)
Tarsus: 1.75cm (0.75in)

Before describing our native Bullfinch we must mention the Northern Bullfinch *(Pyrrhula pyrrhula pyrrhula)* which breeds close to the Arctic Circle in Norway, Sweden, Finland, North Russia, North and South Siberia and down into Eastern Central Asia and parts of Europe. It is much larger (especially in the east) and more brightly coloured than the British bullfinch, and not so aggressive. Otherwise its habits are much the same. The following descriptions refer to our native bullfinch *(P p pileata)*.

Cock
Glossy black crown, nape and chin. Upper parts blue-grey with white rump. Underparts bright pinkish-red, lower belly and undertail white. Primaries and tail blue-black.

Hen
Glossy black crown, nape and chin, but a little duller in these areas than the cock. Upper parts grey-brown with white rump. Underparts vary considerably from greyish brown to a much richer chocolate brown. Vent and undertail white. Primaries and tail black.

Juveniles
Juveniles resemble the hen but they do not have black heads and chins. These come with the first moult, as do the red breasts of the young cocks.

14

Lifestyle in the Wild - Bullfinches

Bill
The bill, black in colour, is shorter and rounder than that of other finches, being better suited to the bullfinches' diet of tree seeds, berries and buds. Because of this, they rarely feed on the ground, where they have some difficulty in picking up seeds.

Legs and Feet
Rather short legs for the size of the bird and smallish feet so that it cannot feed upside down like some finches. Legs and feet are blackish brown.

Crop and Cheek Pouches
Bullfinches do not have storage crops like some finches but in the breeding season cheek pouches develop in the bottom of their mouths each side of their tongues. Bullfinches are highly insectivorous while breeding.

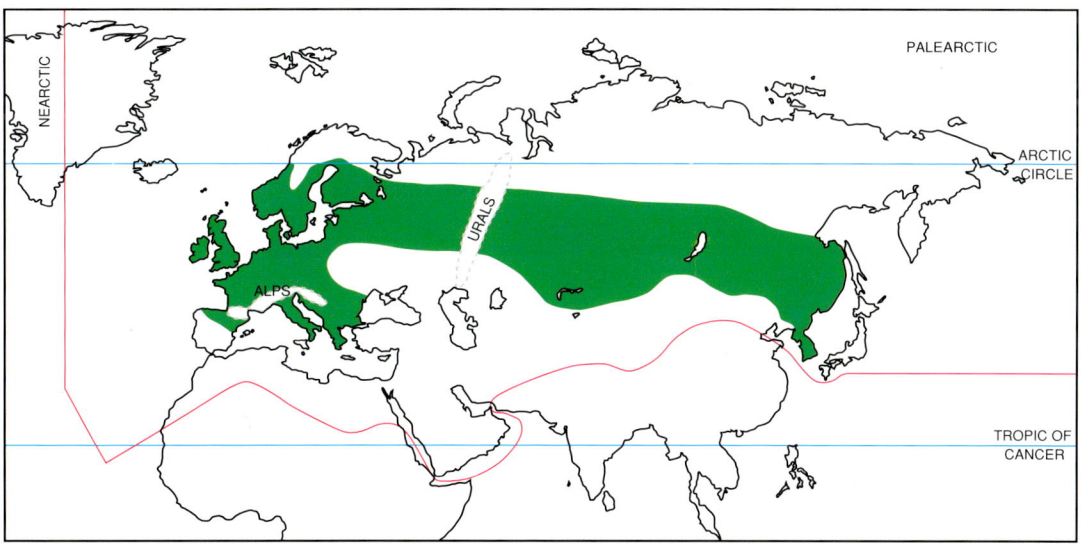

Fig 1: World-wide bullfinch distribution

Most insectivorous birds have to make many journeys to the nest carrying one caterpillar or whatever at a time. The pouches serve the same purpose as the crop in other finches and enable the birds to make far fewer visits to the nest. At the end of the breeding season the cheek pouches regress.

Distribution
Our native bullfinch is not found outside the British Isles and is rather scarce in some areas of Scotland.

Habitat
Bullfinches inhabit woods, shrubberies, thickets and old hedgerows where there is an undergrowth of thorns and plenty of dense, tall cover, though they will often feed outside their territory in gardens and orchards.

Chapter 3

Migration
Although the northern bullfinch is a partial migrant, our native bullfinch never goes more than a few miles from its territory in either summer or winter. Even juveniles when they disperse after moulting will rarely be found more than 25 miles from where they were reared.

Flight
Their flight is the usual undulating flight of the finches, but bullfinches are seldom seen far from cover, and generally in pairs or family parties in the autumn, always keeping in touch with each other with a low, piping call.

Lifespan
The bullfinch is heavily predated both by man and natural enemies; consequently only a small proportion live to breed. In addition they suffer heavy losses in the winter through shortage of food. Those that do survive probably live two to three years at most.

Main Foods
Throughout the winter their main foods are ash keys and other tree fruits but, when these are exhausted in spring, they turn to such foods as the buds of the hawthorn, blackthorn, oak, crab apple, pear, apple, plum, gooseberry and currants until the new vegetation is seeding. Seeds of ripe and semi-ripe groundsel, chickweed, dandelion, dog's mercury, Jack-by-the-hedge, buttercup, sowthistle, docks and charlock will all be taken. In the breeding season such small creatures as caterpillars, spiders, aphids, and small snails form the main part of their diet. In the autumn and winter bullfinches feast by extracting seeds from the fruits of blackberries, privet, elder and mountain ash as well as from nettles, docks, meadowsweet and other plants still holding seed.

Flocking
Bullfinches do not flock like other finches; they pair-bond, usually for life, and the bonded pair stay together throughout the year. In the autumn, small family parties of six to eight may be seen, but by December the young have been driven away to find their own territories. During late autumn and winter they will often join with other bullfinches in parties of 30 or 40 and more to feed on neutral ground. These parties will follow a similar feeding pattern each day until the food supply is exhausted.

Courtship and Territory
When looking for a mate both cocks and hens will sing a subdued jangling sub-song. Apart from this they only ever utter the piping call note and do not have a strong song, like many of the Carduelis finches. The cock will face the hen, puffing out his red breast feathers while twisting and bowing his tail from side to side. The hen will vibrate, with drooping wings and spreading tail. The cock is rather slow to mate and the hen has to be very patient.

Fig 2: The bullfinch in the British Isles

Lifestyle in the Wild - Bullfinches

The pair establish a territory in which they live throughout the year. When breeding both cocks and hens will fight like demons, sometimes to the death, if they feel their territory is threatened by an interloper. The territory has to be large enough for them to find sufficient food to raise a family.

Nesting
Bullfinches are very secretive birds at this time and the nest is usually well hidden in thick cover. The cock stays well away from it to avoid giving away its position, except when he is bringing food. The nest is usually about one or two metres from the ground in thick hedges, clumps of evergreen such as conifer, yew or plantations. It is built by the hen on a foundation of a few fine twigs, with a layer of interlacing fine roots and sometimes moss or lichens. There is not much lining. Some nests are rather poorly built but others are stoutly constructed.

Laying and Incubation
Four to six green-blue eggs with a few dark purple-brown spots and streaks are usually laid in late April or early May. Incubation by the hen starts when the clutch is complete and lasts 13 to 14 days. Although field guide books say that two broods are normal there is some doubt about this. On the other hand, bullfinches are extremely persistent nesters and, if nests are lost or destroyed, they will keep trying until the breeding season comes to an end.

Young
When the young are first hatched the cock brings food for the hen, who feeds the young. As the young grow the hen is able to leave the nest for longer periods. At this time the cock will help to feed the young and she is able to feed herself and bring food for the young, which are fed by regurgitation.

Fledging
The growth of the young depends on how much food the parents are able to find, which varies according to the weather. Fledging takes anything from 12 to 16 days but is generally about 14 days. Even when they are fully feathered the youngsters' tail feathers are not fully grown straight away but are usually full length by the time that they are weaned. The parents will continue to feed the young for about 14 days after they leave the nest. Once self-supporting the young stay with their parents in their territory until after they have moulted out into adult plumage. After this the parents will start to drive them away to find their own territories.

Meadowsweet

Moult
Adult bullfinches moult between August and October and have a complete change of all feathers. The young start to moult at 12 to 14 weeks, coming into adult plumage with black head and chin and red breast in the cocks, but they do not normally moult their wing primaries or their tails until the following year.

The moult is necessary because, after a year, a bird's feathers become worn and are less effective for flight and insulation. In most

Chapter 3

birds the moult occurs outside the breeding and migration seasons but while food is still sufficiently plentiful to support the growth of feathers. However, we do not know exactly what brings on the moult. Reducing daylight length has some effect and perhaps colder nights. Nevertheless, not all birds of any given species finish breeding at the same time, although it is not unknown for a pair to commence a late nest only to abandon it while young are still in the nest and start moulting immediately.

Adult finches replace all their feathers after breeding. Sexual activities cease within a matter of days. The birds become silent and keep mostly in cover. Gonads regress and the sex hormones

Bullfinch cock

are replaced by other hormones. The thyroid hormone raises the birds' metabolic rate and controls the growth of new feathers, which are fed from the blood stream, while the skin becomes heavily vascularised instead of being loose and thin.

Feathers are grouped into tracts that run along the length of the body with bare areas of skin in between, as can easily be seen in nestlings. In nestlings, all the feathers grow at the same time until they spread over the whole body. In adults, new feathers emerge in a regular sequence over a period of several weeks. When one feather is grown, the next is shed, so that the bird is never left naked or unable to fly. If feathers are knocked out accidentally outside the moulting season, replacement feathers grow immediately, but not if a feather is just broken. Each growing feather is encased in a sheath or quill containing blood. When the feather is about one third grown it breaks the sheath, which shrinks and finally drops away. Within a few days of the feather completing its growth it hardens, the blood supply stops, and it becomes a dead structure held by the muscles at its base.

In adult finches the first feathers to be shed are the innermost primaries and the outermost secondaries of both wings, the last in each wing being the outermost primaries and the innermost secondaries. The large tail feathers are moulted in pairs, beginning with the central pair. Body feathers are moulted from the centre of each feather tract spreading outwards. In their first moult, juveniles retain their large flight and tail feathers for another year. Apart from this they moult their feathers in the same sequence as adults. Most juveniles moult

Lifestyle in the Wild - Bullfinches

when they are about 12 weeks old, but late hatched birds moult before that age, when the adults are moulting.

Feathers consist almost exclusively of keratins, which are proteins containing large amounts of sulphur amino-acids, cystine and methionine. For this reason the birds require a great deal of protein during the moult, which has to come from the food that the birds eat at the time. The true nutritional requirements to provide this are not yet known. The food must be available continuously. Any shortage on even one day is sufficient to cause the formation of a fault bar on the growing feather, which is then liable to break at this point during the year. As well as producing new feathers, the bird loses heat much more easily while moulting and therefore must eat more. Adults generally take up to 12 weeks to moult completely, usually beginning from August to October.

Culed Dock

Feather Type

In most species, including finches, there are two feather types, and a bird has either one or the other.

- A jonque has shorter, narrow, silky feathers that are much better coloured and make the bird look brighter but smaller. This is generally known by aviculturists as a yellow, but this name is very misleading, because it does not refer to the colour of the bird.
- A mealy has longer, broader, coarser feathers, the tips of which are pale buff or white. The bird has a mealy appearance, but looks larger and has a duller appearance than the jonque. This is generally known by aviculturists as a buff, but again it is misleading, because it has no direct connection with the colour of the bird, but with its feather type.

In bullfinch cocks the jonque (yellow/intensive) is easy to distinguish, being a much brighter colour and having smoother, neater feather; the mealy (buff/non-intensive) is a larger bird with less colour and slightly coarser looking feathers. Both types exist in the hen but are not so easy to identify without experience because the difference in the colour is not always so obvious. However, the jonque feather type hen is usually smaller and of a rich brown hue. Mealies are greyer.

Bullfinches as Pests

In many fruit growing areas bullfinches are considered pests because of the damage they do to fruit trees, as they consume large amounts of fruit buds. Each year the Ministry of Agriculture, Fisheries and Food issues licences to various growers or their authorised representatives to capture bullfinches in trap cages. Details of such licences in your county can be obtained from the Ministry or from the Department of the Environment, Wildlife Division, who issue licences permitting licensed trappers to give these birds to aviculturists if they so wish. Certain rules must be obeyed, and such licences are reviewed at regular intervals. These licences place the bullfinch in the same category as species previously included in Part II of Schedule 2 of the Wildlife and Countryside Act 1981.

If bullfinches are given to an aviculturist full details about the person and the number of birds concerned must be sent to the Department of the Environment. Naturally they would not expect any one aviculturist to receive more than one or two pairs, unless these were to be passed to other aviculturists and all the correct procedures followed. Such birds can only be used for breeding and cannot be sold or exhibited, but the young bred from them can, provided that they are ringed with the correct approved ring.

Chapter 4

Accommodation and Foods -
Bullfinches

ACCOMMODATION

There is no doubt that bullfinches breed best in a small aviary on their own, where it is possible to provide the cover they like and they can collect some insects during the breeding season to rear their young. In the breeding season two pairs of bullfinches should never be in sight of one another; otherwise both cocks and hens will spend all day trying to defend territory instead of breeding. They can be bred in a mixed aviary as long as there is more than one other pair of birds. Where there is only one other pair, the bullfinches drive them almost continually and prevent them from feeding. When there are several pairs the bullfinches cannot chase them all at once, but it is essential to have at least two feeding stations. Even then, some bullfinches prove so disruptive to other aviary birds that they have to be removed. Some breeders shorten the main primaries of one wing of the male by clipping them in half, thus curtailing his power of flight.

A convenient size of aviary for a pair of bullfinches is 2m x 1m x 2m (6ft x 3ft x 6ft) and some protective cover for the food should be included. Also it is best to put some cover over the nesting area as protection from thunder storms and to provide some shade from the midday sun. Conifer or yew branches are useful for providing the cover necessary for nesting. Bullfinches take readily to small wicker baskets provided that they are well hidden, and this is a great help, particularly with hens that construct only flimsy nests. Always bear in mind the need to get to the nest to ring the young with as little disturbance as possible. Bullfinches generally resent interference in the nest and it is best to watch from a distance to see when they are building and to look out for egg shells to know when the young have hatched so that you can work out when they should be ringed. Some hens will tolerate discreet inspections, but it is really a case of knowing your birds.

An overgrown floor with nettles and long grasses on which the birds will find quantities of small insects is a great help. Rambling roses can be grown up the outside of the aviary and will attract a lot of greenfly, some of which the birds will catch. Roses and other shrubs cannot be grown inside the aviary because the birds will kill the plants by taking all the buds. Much depends on the size of the aviary. Given enough space some shrubs can survive the predation of the

Accommodation and Foods - Bullfinches

birds but they need to be hardy, vigorous varieties such as elderberry and blackberry, and these need regularly pruning to prevent them from damaging the wire of the structure.

Notwithstanding the above remarks, bullfinch hens nest readily in large cages when used for breeding mules or hybrids. The difficulty lies in rearing the young in such accommodation because of the live food required. For this reason, such mules and hybrids are usually fostered to and reared by canaries or greenfinches on egg food, both species usually proving excellent foster parents. If the bullfinches can be persuaded to take canary egg food with a hard boiled egg mixed into it, plus mealworms and the usual seeding weeds, they can rear their own young. Some bullfinches are excellent parents, but it has to be said that many are not, so it may well be necessary to resort to foster parents.

Bullfinch hen

Chapter 4

It has to be said that canaries and greenfinches are not so reliable when it comes to fostering pure-bred bullfinch chicks. Many would-be foster parents seem to have difficulties in managing them, and it is not just a matter of dietary needs. Newly-hatched bullfinch chicks have brightly coloured gapes to which some foster parents seem to object. Also, when they are small their heads weave and wobble all over the place, considerably more than many other species of finch, and the foster parents need an abundance of patience to cope with them. Some foster parents manage to get them over this stage only to lose them when they fledge and leave the nest. Because of their different begging action and stance, many foster parents just do not seem able to wean them successfully. Hand rearing can be resorted to at any stage from hatching to weaning. They are not particularly difficult in this respect, especially now we have so many good proprietary hand rearing foods on the market, but hand rearing requires time and patience and should not be undertaken lightly; it is perhaps best considered as a last resort.

Do not let any of this put you off breeding bullfinches. Given suitable accommodation and proper attention to dietary needs they can be reliable and at times prolific breeders - a challenging but rewarding species.

Coltsfoot

FOODS

When it comes to feeding we need to bear in mind that bullfinches are considerably different to Carduelis finches such as greenfinches and goldfinches. This is another reason, quite apart from their territorial aggression, for keeping them apart from other species. Particular attention to dietary needs is necessary if these birds are to thrive. The species is very susceptible to a respiratory problem caused by a mycoplasma, resulting in laboured breathing and gasping, which in turn leads to a general deterioration in health. Incorrect diet, including too much sunflower and hemp seed, seems to induce or aggravate the disease. The disease can be treated effectively with the drug Tylosin but prevention should be the aim as the drug only alleviates the problem. The disease will quickly take hold again if steps are not taken to correct the cause of the problem. A sensible and varied diet, plenty of exercise and fresh air will go a long way in prevention of this disease.

Seed

The basic seed mixture needs to be fairly plain. Many seed merchants will make up a British finch mixture without hemp if asked. The mix should consist of equal parts of plain canary seed, black and red rape with half part linseed, niger, teasel and Japanese millet to which should be added half part British condition seed, preferably one which does not contain hemp or contains only a trace of this seed. Seeds listed below should be fed in small amounts regularly.

Hemp: As stated before, this seed should be avoided or fed very sparingly for most of the year, but it is useful in the rearing period if boiled or soaked for chiting (sprouting). It should only be boiled for a minute or two.
Sunflower: Again this should be fed sparingly. Three or four seeds of the small striped variety are ample. The amount can be increased during the rearing period if they are soaked for chiting.

Accommodation and Foods - Bullfinches

Perilla: A very useful seed that can be fed in reasonable amounts. It is said to have medicinal properties.
Pine Nuts: The small Chinese variety is favoured and can be fed in small amounts.
Gold of Pleasure: This small seed is best fed separately in small quantities. It is a fine conditioner.
Maw Seed: This is an excellent conditioner, often taken in large amounts with beneficial results by any bird that is a little off colour. Being very small it is best supplied in a separate pot.
Soaked Seeds: Wild birds normally eat seeds while they are ripening and hard dried seeds are generally unnatural. Seeds that have been soaked in water for 24 hours help to overcome this and should be fed regularly especially in the breeding season. The water must be changed several times during that period so that the seeds do not go sour. Rinse well and allow the water to drain off before feeding. A teaspoonful of bleach per litre of water kills harmful bacteria and prevents the seed from smelling.

Grit

Grit is an important part of every finch's diet and enables their gizzards to grind up the seeds that they eat. Supply a good quality mineralised grit suitable for cage birds, regularly.

Greenfood

Greenfood should be offered regularly. Greenleaf and seeds, semi-ripe and ripe, will be taken from lettuce, spinach and all the brassica family. Also useful are wild plants such as dandelion, groundsel, chickweed, sow and milk thistle, shepherds purse, persicaria, plantain, docks, stinging nettles and many others, plus favoured spring swelling buds of hawthorn, blackthorn, apple, pear, plum, cherry and others, especially those of the prunus family.

Dandelion

Tree Fruits

Tree fruits in their season should form a regular part of the diet. The bird is after the seeds within the fruit, but in the process of extracting seed considerable amounts of the fruit are consumed. Seasonal favourites are : ashkeys, blackberries and currants (including all their cultivated relatives), elder, rowan, privet, honeysuckle, cotoneaster and snowberry. Some of these can be purchased dried and then soaked before feeding, but there is no doubt that bullfinches favour freshly gathered fruits.

Egg Food

The kind of egg food that is fed to canaries is very beneficial and every effort should be made to persuade bullfinches to take it by keeping canaries with them during the winter months.

Water

A fresh supply daily of good clean water for drinking and bathing is essential. Without water for more than a few hours a bird will die from dehydration. A bath every day, winter and summer, will keep its plumage in good condition. Some breeders recommend rainwater

Chapter 4

where possible because there are chemicals in tap water that they believe may be harmful to the bird's health. Others use filtered tap water. It depends where you live.

Cuttlefish Bone
This supplies calcium and should always be available, although the birds may not take much outside the breeding season.

Live Foods
These are considered essential for bringing the birds into full breeding condition and rearing the young. Small caterpillars, spiders, aphids, flies and small snails are natural rearing foods. Ant eggs are very useful and can be bought dried from pet shops and scalded to swell them. Bullfinches will learn to take mealworms, but these should not be overdone. As with other finches, the supply needs to be regulated.

Blackberry

Supplements
A bird's exact requirements are not known, but few additives are needed if a full and varied diet is provided throughout the year. However, some breeders add various supplements to the main foods in an effort to overcome possible shortages, particularly in vitamins and minerals. Care should be taken not to exceed the recommended quantities.

ABIDEC*: This is a very useful vitamin supplement and is best added to the drinking water. There are many other useful multi-vitamin type supplements on the market, any one of which should meet your birds' needs.

Cod Liver Oil: This is a rich source of vitamin D and can be given throughout the breeding season and during the moult. One teaspoonful is mixed thoroughly with one pound of seed, which is allowed to stand for 24 hours before being fed to the birds.

PYM*: Yeast can be mixed with seed in almost any quantities, as can mineral mixtures, especially those containing iodine. These are a good help in maintaining healthy condition.

Tonics: These can be useful, especially the ones containing iron.

Probiotics: These encourage and build up the 'friendly' bacteria whose function is to keep all the 'unfriendly' bacteria in the gut in check. Probiotics can be given daily throughout the year in the drinking water. (Dosage: according to manufacturers' instructions.)

* Registered Trade Mark

Chapter 5

Breeding -
Bullfinches

Bullfinches are sometimes bred in mixed company aviaries but to be consistently successful each breeding pair will need an aviary, flight or large cage to themselves and success will generally depend on following the bird's natural life style in the wild as far as possible. The information given in chapter 3 should therefore be studied carefully.

Pairing

Bullfinches in the wild pair for life and are devoted to each other, always keeping in touch by means of their piping calls. In aviculture this is not always a practical scenario, particularly if we are trying to form a strain; pairs may need to be broken up after one season, or even part way through a season, and re-paired to suit our programme. However, although the bond is strong whilst they are together, in the wild the species is heavily predated and life can be short. For this reason, if the bond is broken through death or for any other reason, after a short lapse of time a bullfinch will accept or seek out a new partner: a trait we can use to our advantage.

During the autumn and winter, adult bonded pairs from which you intend to breed in the coming season should be kept together either as a single pair or as small groups of four or five bonded pairs in larger aviaries. It is important not to introduce any unattached birds into the group or serious squabbling will ensue, often with fatal results. If one of the group should die or need to be removed it will be necessary to remove the partner also, which should be housed by itself for a while (a few days will suffice) and then put with a new partner to bond or introduced into an unattached group; there may be a little squabbling initially but they will usually settle down.

Young birds of the season and unattached adults can be housed in small groups if given plenty of space. If space allows, unattached birds can be segregated by sex to prevent them forming unwanted relationships. As daylight hours lengthen, around February, the bonded pairs housed in groups will need to be separated and put into breeding quarters by themselves. Groups of unattached birds will become quarrelsome even if the sexes have been segregated; they will now need to be housed as bonded pairs or single individuals if fatalities are to be avoided.

25

Chapter 5

Nesting

To help the birds attain breeding condition, spring swelling tree buds, dandelion (leaf and seeding heads) and other favoured greens and seeding plants, canary rearing food, soaked seed and live food (mealworms will suffice) should all be fed regularly in increasing amounts with the approach of spring. Both sexes will begin to utter their 'whirred' piping song, but the cocks are more vociferous. They will start to carry small twigs, roots and fibres about. Earnest nest building will usually start in April, depending on the weather. Nesting sites as described in chapter 1 should be provided. Bullfinches are not particularly fussy but like to feel secure, so should be given a reasonable amount of cover. Do not make the cover so thick that the nesting site is too dark; bear in mind that they do not like interference, especially when young have hatched.

Fine twigs of birch, blackthorn or similar should be provided for the base, and coconut fibre and fine roots for the lining. A lilac tree provides plenty of fine roots or you can lift a tussock of coarse grass and wash the soil away to reveal an abundance of them. A few hairs may also be used to line the nest, which can be a substantial or flimsy affair. Most hens will take to a small wicker basket, thus avoiding the problem of eggs falling through a poorly constructed nest. Eggs will usually number four to six Some hens are prone to laying eggs on the floor or off the perch; if this happens, a dummy egg placed in the nest after the first mishap will sometimes encourage her onto the nest to lay the rest of the clutch. Some bullfinch hens can appear to be in distress when laying but they are usually best left alone at this time. A sensible and varied diet will go a long way in preventing such problems.

Goldfinch x bullfinch hybrid cock

Breeding - Bullfinches

Brooding

The hen usually goes broody and starts to sit after laying three or four eggs, but sometimes not until she has completed the clutch. She loses the inner layer of feathers on her breast, which allows direct contact between her bare skin and the eggs, thus raising their temperature. The eggs normally hatch in 14 days but there is some variation depending on the weather conditions, particularly temperature. During this time the cock,

Pastel northern bullfinch cock

Chapter 5

although attentive, keeps away from the nest except when bringing food for the hen. He usually sits some distance away, piping his tune.

Rearing bullfinches can be timid and do not like interference, especially when they have newly-hatched young, and it can cause them to desert the nest. Later, when the young are well grown, their calling usually persuades the parents to go on feeding them. In the early stages the cock fills his pouches with insects and other items of food. These are then fed by regurgitation to the hen, who in turn feeds the young. The hen continues brooding until the young are large enough to evacuate onto the rim of the nest, generally at about seven days old. Until that time the hen cleans out the nest. At this stage both the cock and the hen will forage and feed the young by regurgitation. During rearing a regular supply of live food, canary rearing food, soaked seeds and greenfoods in the form of their favoured seeding plants must be provided.

Honeysuckle

Fledging

The young fledge at approximately 14 days old, depending how well the parents have fed them. They look very much like the hen, but without the black on their heads and chins. The cock continues to feed them for about 14 days, after which time they become self-supporting. After weaning the young can usually be left with their parents for several weeks, space permitting. However, under domestic conditions the species is usually double- and even treble-brooded, so it may become necessary to remove the young to a nursery pen when they are fully self-supporting to give a subsequent nest of young a better chance of being reared successfully. Some cocks can be aggressive to their self-supporting young in a confined space, making it necessary to remove them. In any case, they will usually need to be moved to other quarters prior to the moult; towards the end of the breeding season the adult pair will try to drive them out of their territory and, if they are not removed, fatalities will result.

Moulting

The first brood of young will start to moult at about 12 weeks old, later broods a little earlier. Adults will moult any time between late July and October. During this time their diet should be supplemented with a good supply of their favoured feeds of berries and wild plants in season to achieve a good clean moult. These natural foods will help to maintain the natural colours of the birds but, to achieve really good colour, the use of Caraphyll Red* will be found advantageous. Infuse a quarter of a teaspoonful of Caraphyll Red with a little boiling water in a suitable container. Dilute this by adding about one litre of cold water, and mix thoroughly. This diluted mixture is given to the birds in place of normal drinking water throughout the moult and should be made freshly each day.

* Registered Trade Mark of Roche Products Ltd

Privet

Chapter 6

Lifestyle in the Wild -
Chaffinches

Order: Passeriformes
Family: Fringillidae (Finches)
Genus: *Fringilla*
Species: *Fringilla coelebs gengleri*
Common name: British Chaffinch

Description
Length: 15.25cm (6in)
Weight: 21.26g (0.75oz)
Wing Span: 20.25cm (8in)
Tarsus: 1.75cm (0.75in)

Cock
Brownish slate-grey head and nape with reddish-brown back and olive green rump. A broad white shoulder patch with a less prominent whitish wing-bar behind it. Head feathers can be raised to give a slight crest. The cheeks, throat and breast are pinkish orange merging to creamy-white on the lower belly. Wings mainly brownish-black edged green. Slightly forked blackish tail with conspicuous white on outer feathers. In breeding condition the forehead becomes blackish and the crown and nape are a bright slate-blue and the mantle becomes chestnut. The breast assumes a brighter pink.

Hen
The hen is slightly smaller and much duller, lacking the blue cap and pink breast. Upper parts greyish-brown and under parts a rich shade of grey, but with the broad white shoulder-patch and wing-bar similar to that of the cock but not so well defined. Easy to sex.

Juveniles
Juveniles are like the hen, but with less green on the rump.

Bill
Thick, tapering to a sharp point. In the cock, whitish-brown with a dark tip in winter turning to bright steel-blue in the breeding season. Hen and juveniles beaks are brown and paler underneath.

29

Chapter 6

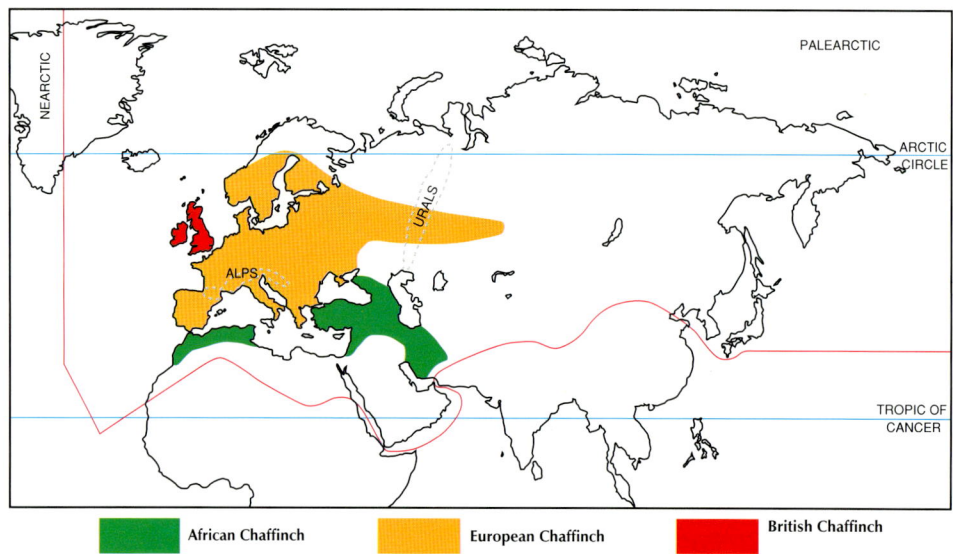

Chaffinch distribution world-wide

Legs and Feet
Pale brown. Chaffinches and bramblings have longer legs than many other finches and, unlike *Carduelis* and *Pyrrhula* finches, can walk and run, although they still frequently prefer to hop. Apart from catching insects in the breeding season, they normally feed on the ground, not clinging to food plants like many other finches.

Distribution
Abundantly and widely distributed throughout the British Isles. The European chaffinch breeds throughout Europe generally, south Norway, up to the tree-line in Finland and Russia, and western Asia.

Habitat
Gardens, hedgerows, thickets and bushy commons, deciduous and coniferous woods and copses. Outside the breeding season it can also be found in stubbles, root fields and stackyards.

Migration
The British chaffinch is resident and ringing returns show that it rarely moves more than 10 miles from where it was born. The European chaffinch, however, migrates west in the autumn and large flocks arrive on the east coast of Great Britain from September onwards and continue to move in a westerly direction. There is a tendency for the flocks to segregate sexually, hens tending to travel further west than cocks. Return migrations take place in March and April. There is no evidence of interbreeding with the British race in the wild state.

Flight
Typical undulating finch flight, but generally does not call in the air.

Lifestyle in the Wild - Chaffinches

Lifespan
Ringing returns suggest that chaffinches that survive their first winter live for two-and-a-half years on average, rather longer than most British finches. This is supported by the fact that they are generally single brooded.

Main Foods
In the breeding season chaffinches are almost entirely insectivorous, feeding on caterpillars, insects, small flies, moths and butterflies, beetles, earwigs and spiders. Beech mast is a favourite food in winter as are the seed of elderberry together with cereal grains and common weeds such as brassicas, goosefoots, persicaria and chick-weeds. They feed mainly on the ground.

Flocking
British Chaffinch: Several families, both cocks and hens, join together in small flocks of a dozen or so in winter.
European Chaffinch: Large flocks are formed, mainly of one sex only, in which they migrate to their winter quarters.

Courtship and Territory
Being insectivorous, chaffinches need and defend a fairly large territory, the size of which depends on the particular habitat and the availability of food within the territory. In the spring the cock takes up a territory and sings from all convenient song posts, both to defend the territory from other males and to attract females. As they are coming into breeding condition the hens visit different cocks until they find one who takes their fancy. Sexual flights then take place - swerving, headlong chases with the cock following close behind the hen. These are followed by the cock drooping and fluttering wings and spreading his tail. In between times the cock will sing loudly from a nearby song post. When she is ready the hen will invite coition with shivering wings and raised tail.

Nesting
Chaffinches build the most beautiful nests of all the British finches. These are generally at no great height and nearly always in a fork of a tree or shrub. Breeding can begin in mid-April while the trees are still quite bare. The nest is made of grasses, roots, wool and moss and decorated externally with lichens, birch-bark or fragments of paper, fastened together with spiders webs and lined with hair. It is well and compactly built and so well camouflaged that it is easy to walk past without seeing it. Perhaps this is the reason why chaffinches do not seem to be predated as much as some other finches.

Chaffinches in the British Isles

Chapter 6

Laying and Incubation
Four or five greenish-blue eggs with very dark purplish-brown spots and streaks are generally laid in early May. Incubation by the hen starts when the clutch is complete and lasts about 13 days. The cock feeds the hen while she is sitting. He does not have a crop like some finches and has to make frequent journeys with insects.

Young
When the young are first hatched the cock feeds the hen and the hen feeds the young. The hen continues to brood the young until they are half grown and will then help the cock to bring food, both making up to 20 visits per hour to the nest. Nesting is timed to coincide with the main caterpillar period and there is generally only one brood. In the southern part of their range they may have a second nest if food is plentiful.

Silver birch

Chaffinch cock

Fledging
At about 14 days old the young are well grown and fully feathered. At this stage they leave the nest although the parents continue to feed them for another two weeks. By then they are self-supporting.

Moult
The juveniles start to moult in July in the same way as other finches (see chapter 3), retaining their flight and tail feathers until the following year. The parents start their moult from July onwards when they have finished breeding.

Feather Type
(See chapter 3) There are both jonque (intensive) (yellow) and mealy (non-intensive) (buff) feather types, but these are more easily distinguishable in cocks than hens.

Chapter 7

Lifestyle in the Wild -
Bramblings

Order: Passeriformes
Family: Fringillidae (finches)
Genus: *Fringilla*
Species: *Fringilla montifringilla*
Common Name: Brambling (Bramblefinch)

Description
    Length: 15cm (5.75in)
    Weight: 21.26g (0.75oz)
    Wing Span: 20.25cm (8in)
    Tarsus: 1.75cm (0.75in)

Cock
Same general shape as the chaffinch but a little more robust looking and with a slightly shorter tail. Mainly orange-buff colouration with flecked flanks. Head mottled with brown on black. Like the chaffinch it is able to raise the head feathers to a slight crest. Throat and breast orange-buff shading to white on the belly. Dark brown wings with orange-buff shoulder-patch and conspicuous white rump. Dark brown distinctly forked tail. In the breeding season the cock assumes a completely black head, mantle, wings and tail.

Hen
Dull brown upper parts, wings and tail, buff grey head, paler orange on throat and breast and shoulder-patch. An easy bird to sex.

Juveniles
Like the hen but much paler throughout. Mottled on mantle.

Bill
Thick, tapering gradually to a point and slightly larger than the chaffinch's bill. Colour yellow but in the breeding season the cock's bill turns blackish.

33

Chapter 7

Legs and Feet
Brownish flesh colour. Like the chaffinch, the brambling has longer legs than many other finches, enabling it to walk and run. Bramblings normally feed on the ground and do not often cling to food plants.

Distribution
The brambling breeds to the tree limit along the Arctic Circle in Norway, Finland, Russia and Siberia and south into Northern Europe in a narrow zone where it overlaps the chaffinch. In winter it moves south into the whole of Europe and most of Asia. Varying numbers visit the British Isles in winter, depending on the weather and available food supplies.

Habitat
In the breeding season, mainly sub-Arctic birch woods, open conifer forests and sometimes in tall willow scrub on the Tundra. In the winter, mainly beech and deciduous woods with rowan trees.

Migration
The brambling is a true migrant species and in the autumn it completely vacates its breeding area. Travelling generally by night it is audible in flight. It moves south and west until it finds beech mast and rowan berries, moving on when the supply is exhausted until it finds another crop. This results in huge concentrations wherever there is a good crop.

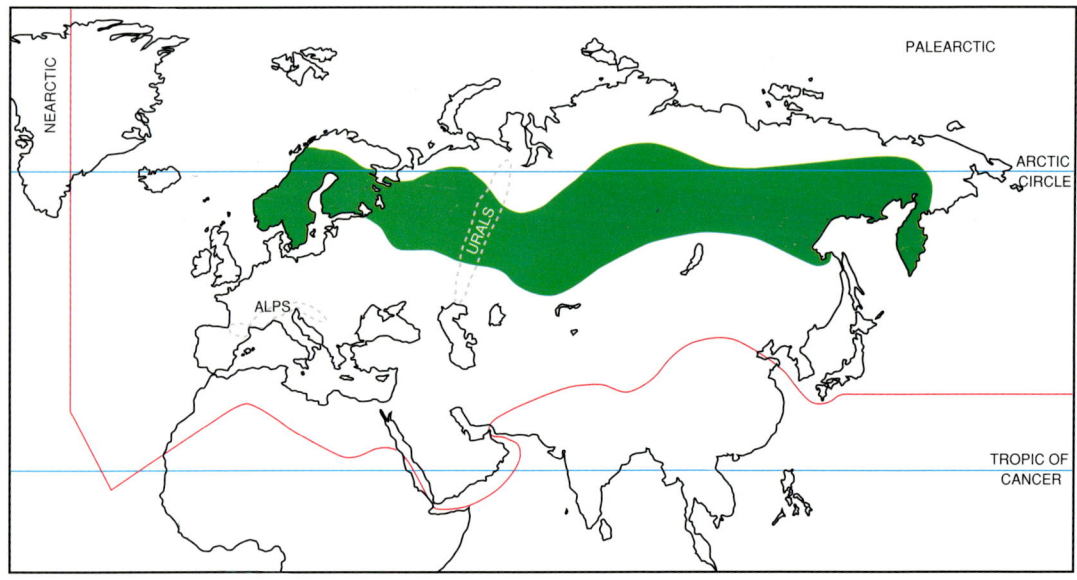

Brambling distribution world-wide

Lifestyle in the Wild - Bramblings

Flight
Similar to the chaffinch's undulating flight but stronger and faster.

Lifespan
Very little information is available on the lifespan of the brambling but it is probably similar to that of the chaffinch, averaging about two-and-a-half years for birds that survive their first winter.

Main Foods
In winter their main foods are without doubt beech mast and rowan berries. In the breeding season bramblings are almost totally insectivorous, feeding on caterpillars, insects, small flies, moths and butterflies, beetles, earwigs and spiders, but they also take some conifer seeds which they are able to obtain with their large beaks. While moving from one beech crop to the next, like the chaffinch they will feed on stubble fields, where they eat cereal grains and common weed seeds.

Mountain Ash

Flocking
This only takes place during migration and throughout the winter.
Some very large flocks are seen, sometimes mixed with other finches, especially chaffinches.

Courtship and Territory
Throughout the breeding season the brambling is very territorial and its behaviour is very similar to that of the chaffinch both in territory and courtship.

Nesting
The nest is similar to that of the chaffinch but larger and less well finished with stouter and deeper walls, built in birches and conifers and usually 2.5-3.5m (5-10ft) from the ground. It is built of grasses, roots, wool and moss, generally decorated with pieces of birch bark and lichens. The lining is hair, feathers and sometimes down. Breeding commences mid-May to early June. Bramblings are generally single brooded but in the southern part of their range they sometimes have two broods.

Laying and Incubation
Generally five or six eggs, but sometimes seven, make up the clutch. They are similar to chaffinch eggs but slightly darker and greener. Incubation by the hen alone commences when the clutch is nearing completion and takes approximately 14 days. The cock feeds the hen while she is sitting and she only leaves the nest for very short spells once or twice a day.

Young
The cock brings food and the hen feeds the young for the first few days after they are hatched. As the young grow the hen will leave the nest for longer periods and help the cock to forage for food. After about seven

Chapter 7

Brambling cock

days the hen will cease to brood except at night and both parents will then feed the young. Being insectivorous like the chaffinch, they have to make numerous journeys with food continually throughout the day. They do not have crops like some of the finches and are unable to bring more than one beakful at a time.

Fledging
The young are fully grown and fledge at about 14 days old, but the parents continue to feed them for another two weeks.

Moult
Bramblings moult early, starting in late July or August, so that they have their new feathers before they migrate. As with other species (see chapter 3) the young do not moult their primaries and tail feathers until the following year.

Feather Type
(See chapter 3) Both jonque (intensive) (yellow) and mealy (non-intensive) (buff) feather types exist, and it is generally easy to recognise them in both cocks and hens.

Chapter 8

Accommodation and Foods -
Chaffinches and Bramblings

The chaffinch and brambling are alike in so many ways that under domestic conditions they can be treated as one and the same. Given suitable housing and feeding, they are undoubtedly the hardiest and longest lived of our British hardbills. There are many instances of them reaching 15 years of age and they have been known to live 20 years or more.

ACCOMMODATION

In housing these birds it has to be remembered that the males are highly territorial in the breeding season and their courtship is of a vigorous nature. Hens will need space and cover to escape the ardent attentions of the cock. Otherwise, they present few problems. Non-breeding birds can be caged individually and will keep in good condition, but the cage should not be less than 1m (3ft) in length. During the autumn and winter they can be caged in pairs (cock and hen) in large cages if necessary but, unless there is some specific reason for doing so, such as for training for exhibition, they are best housed in aviaries. Given enough space, they can be kept in small groups. Sexes can be segregated but it is not really necessary.

As daylight hours begin to lengthen, the cocks will start to come into breeding condition. Those in groups will then need to be separated or fatalities will soon follow. Given enough space some pairs can be left in mixed collections with *Carduelis* finches but must be reduced to only one pair of either chaffinch or brambling. Cocks of either species that can be trusted in mixed collections at breeding time are the exception rather than the rule. The vast majority will become far too aggressive towards other birds in the collection. Some breeders get over the problem to some extent by shortening the main primaries of one wing to curtail the cock bird's power of flight.

Without doubt, these two species do best in a small aviary to themselves just before and during the breeding season, but the need for access to ring the young must not be forgotten. An ideal size is 2m x 2m x 2m (6ft x 6ft x 6ft). Birds of both species will build a natural nest in a fork, so plenty of forked branches should be provided. A useful arrangement that is nearly always accepted is to fix a good forked branch about 1.5m above the ground and another branch horizontally through the fork, but they will usually accept whatever is provided in the way of baskets, bowls and pans (see chapter 1). They are not too fussy and very little cover is required for the nest (a few evergreen twigs will suffice) but it should be shaded from the midday sun and protected from thunderstorms. On the other hand, some natural cover should be provided within the aviary so that the hen can get away from the cock

Chapter 8

Brambling hen

when necessary during the pre-mating period. A patch of nettles, a pile of stable manure and some rotting fruit in a suitable receptacle will enable the birds to find quite a lot of insects for themselves. This keeps them occupied and in good condition as well as being very helpful when they have young to feed.

FOODS
Both species are fairly coarse feeders. A good British finch seed mixture to which has been added a little good quality British bird condition seed will serve well enough as a basic diet, to which should be added small amounts of useful favoured seeds and other foods.

Seeds
Hemp: This is useful and well liked, but it is more economical if fed separately; otherwise the birds will waste a considerable amount of the mixture while looking for the hemp seeds.
Pine Nuts: The small Chinese ones are similar to their natural winter diet and highly nutritious.
Sunflower: Small striped sunflowers are both popular and nutritious particularly if soaked.
Groats: Another near-natural food particularly useful in the winter.
Niger: This is included in most mixtures but is nourishing and helps to bring the birds into breeding condition if increased in the winter and early spring months.
Maw and Gold of Pleasure: These seeds, being very small, are best fed separately. Both are reputed to have some medicinal properties.

Perilla: A useful, nourishing seed that seems to help prevent and correct digestive upsets.
Soaked Seed Mixture: Chaffinches and bramblings are ground-feeding species in the wild, so seeds softened by the vagaries of the weather are a natural feed. Small amounts should be given regularly in a separate dish or mixed with soft foods. See chapter 4 for the method of soaking.

Green Food
Neither species show much of a liking for green foods. A little grated carrot and finely chopped lettuce, spinach or brassica can be added to whatever soft foods are being fed. The birds will keenly peck over wild foods such as chickweed in search of tiny invertebrates, so the provision of such plants is beneficial although very little of the actual plants will be eaten.

Soft Foods
It is important to get the birds used to egg food (canary rearing foods). If your birds will not take it, you may have to keep a canary with them during the winter to help achieve this. Give it to them twice a week during winter, increasing to a daily feed in spring. During March start adding finely-chopped hard-boiled egg. Some grated cheddar cheese can also be added. Egg and cheese are the nearest alternative to the animal protein that they obtain from insects in the wild. The egg food can be further improved with the addition of some dried insects. Nowadays, there is an ever-increasing choice of proprietary brands of supplementary foods containing various dried insects, from ants eggs and termites to crickets, beetles and shrimps.

Live Food
In addition to the soft foods, the birds will need supplies of live insects: unlimited when rearing young, one or two daily at other times. Maggots are not recommended these days because there have been losses on a number of occasions due to botulism. Wax moth larvae, mealworms, buffalo worms, white worms and crickets in various stages of growth are readily available. Any caterpillars, beetles, earwigs, spiders and other creepy-crawlies you can catch will be beneficial and add variety.

Water
Good, clean fresh water for drinking and bathing is most important and must be supplied daily. Use rain water if possible because tap water has many chemicals added to it.

Grit
A good mineral grit should always be available, although they may not take much, especially in the breeding season.

Charlock

Cuttlefish Bone
This supplies calcium for the formation of egg shells and helps to prevent rickets in the young by promoting bone growth. It should always be available.

Chapter 9

Breeding -
Chaffinches and Bramblings

Neither species is particularly difficult to breed given suitable accommodation and attention to their dietary needs. Study the birds' natural life styles described in chapters 6 and 7 and follow these as far as is practicable within the domestic conditions provided.

Pairing

The cocks of both species can be vicious at this time, not only with each other and birds of other species but also with hens of their own kind. Care needs to be taken when cock and hen are introduced to each other. If not introduced until the approach to the breeding season they may prove incompatible or the cock may be more forward in condition than the hen. If this is the case some cocks can be unmerciful in driving a reluctant hen. It is far better if each pair is selected and kept together in the autumn and winter, well before the breeding season. They will get to know each other and come into breeding condition more or less simultaneously. This has the effect of taking the steam out of the situation and they will generally settle down well together when put into their breeding enclosure.

Nesting

Assuming the birds have been brought into breeding condition by providing them with additional small and regular amounts of soft and live food they will usually start nest building late April or May. Provide plenty of damp mosses, fine roots and grasses, coconut fibre and other suitable nesting materials, together with dog hair, small feathers and white cotton kapok or similar. Be careful to avoid anything which may contain nylon fibres, as these can cause serious injury to the birds. Nests can take some time to construct. The chaffinch's is a particularly neat affair, the brambling's a little less so and more bulky.

Brooding

Some hens may have a finished nest several days prior to laying; much depends on the prevailing weather at the time. Incubation will usually start in earnest soon after the third egg has been laid. Both species are generally tight sitters and incubation is usually carried out uneventfully. However, a par-

Breeding - Chaffinches and Bramblings

Chaffinch hen

ticularly virile cock can be troublesome in trying to drive his hen to nest again. Sometimes it is possible to run two hens with such cocks to ease the situation but often his ardent pursuits of the second hen will upset the sitting hen, causing her to desert. Such cocks are best removed once the hen is sitting. Hens are usually quite capable of rearing on their own; in fact chaffinch hens are very 'paternal' and will often feed any youngster that begs for food. Once he has been removed it will rarely be practical to reintroduce the cock until the young are self-supporting and can be removed prior to his reintroduction. Both species tend to be single-brooded anyway, but they can be double- and even treble-brooded. Much seems to depend on the individuality of the hen and the availability of live food. Having said this, most cocks of both species are excellent parents who carry out their feeding duties at every opportunity and in an exemplary fashion.

Chapter 9

Canary x bullfinch mule

Rearing

Incubation lasts about 13 days, but hatching can take place as early as 10 days, so make sure plenty of live and soft food is provided from about the 10-day stage of incubation. For the first few days after hatching they will require unlimited amounts of small flies, aphids, white worms, buffalo worms, and mini mealworms. As the chicks grow, larger live foods will be taken in the form of waxworms, mealworms and small crickets plus any spiders earwigs, smooth caterpillars, woodlice and similar that can be gathered. Commercially produced live foods such as mealworms and crickets will need to be dusted with a vitamin powder containing a calcium supplement or fed on one of the specially prepared foods developed for this purpose to avoid deficiency problems. Although high in protein they are lacking in calcium.

Fledging

The young fledge at about 14 days old and the parents, particularly the cock, will continue to feed them for a further 14 days or so. The supply of soft and live foods must be kept up until the young are fully weaned and taking increasing amounts of seeds in their diet. At this stage both can be reduced substantially, although small amounts should be supplied daily until they have completed their moult.

If possible the young are best left with their parents until they have moulted but, if the parents start a second nest or the cock becomes aggressive to them, they should be removed to other quarters as soon as they are seen to be self-supporting. Fortunately, young self-supporting chaffinches and bramblings rarely suffer ill effects when removed from their parents. They can be housed several to an aviary or flight or one or two birds to a roomy cage, the latter being more appropriate if you intend to exhibit the birds at some future date, as it will provide an opportunity to show train them. They can be housed in this fashion until they have completed the moult if necessary.

Sow thistle

Moult

Both species are termed early moulters and usually start moulting in July or early August. Their moult follows the normal pattern of finches (see chapter 3), but they are noted for the speed at which they are capable of moulting. Neither species needs to be colour fed but should be provided with small daily amounts of soft foods and live foods to bring out the best of colour in them.

Colour Feeding

Some breeders do give Caraphyl Red* but, if too much is given, it can discolour them, becoming a disadvantage rather than an advantage on the show bench.

* Registered trade mark of Roche products

Chapter 10

Ringing

The bullfinch, chaffinch and brambling are all on Schedule 3 Part 1 of the Wild Life and Countryside Act 1981. For this reason, although it is permissible to keep them if they are not ringed, it is illegal to buy, sell or exhibit unringed specimens. The bullfinch, which is regarded as a pest by fruit growers because of the damage it can do to fruit trees, is also on Schedule 2 Part 2 of the same act, so has a slightly different status; wild birds taken captive under special licence can be kept by aviculturists for breeding purposes only, but their offspring can be sold or exhibited provided they are ringed with the correct ring. There are two approved legal rings:

- The British Bird Council ring, which is exclusive to the British Bird fancy.
- The IOA ring, which is used for different types of birds and by exhibitors who may wish to send their birds to shows abroad. At present, quarantine and import/export regulations make exhibiting abroad very difficult. However, closer ties with Europe could see some beneficial changes in the regulations in the near future.

The British Bird Council ring is brown, and the letters 'BC' are stamped across it, followed by a size letter and serial number. Since 1991 rings also carry a year date. Much has been done over the years to find the best size for each species, and for the three species under discussion these are:

- Bullfinch: code size D
- Chaffinch: code size C
- Brambling: code size D

This ring has to be put on the young bird while it is still in the nest and is acceptable to the authorities as proof that the bird is aviary-bred.

One problem with the closed ring is that some birds resent either the interference in the nest or the foreign object on the chicks. For this reason, the parent birds must be accustomed to the owner and, if possible, reasonably tame before the breeding season. Bullfinches have given many breeders cause for concern in the past and, to some extent, still do. They often desert or eject their young after ringing or, even worse, mutilate them in an attempt to remove the rings. However, the recent increase of the size of the ring to be fitted to bullfinches from a size C to size D, allowing chicks to be ringed some two days later than previously, has gone some way towards alleviating the problems.

Ringing

Bullfinch chicks can now be ringed at six or even seven days old, depending on their rate of growth and the experience of the ringer. Bramblings can be left a similar length of time, as they also take size D rings. For some reason chaffinches, although much the same size as the other two species, take size C rings: it is thought that this may be based on records of some very small-footed chaffinch hens. For this reason, they have to be ringed at five days at the latest. Fortunately, there is nowhere near as much likelihood of problems with the chaffinch or the brambling as with the bullfinch. A hen is less likely to react adversely if ringing can be left until the young have begun to void their faeces over the side of the nest (about the seven-day mark), so that the she does not have to clear these away and is therefore not so meticulous about keeping her nest 'clean'. Bear in mind that rings that are fitted too early come off in the nest and are lost. If the ring can be removed easily after fitting it is best to leave it for a further day or two. This can arise particularly when the growth of chicks is staggered because they have hatched on different days.

It is still best to err on the side of caution, particularly when the mothers are young or newly-purchased hens whose attitude to rings is unknown. There are usually fewer problems with owner-bred hens than with bought-in stock. When the task of ringing needs to be carried out, give the pair some of their favourite seeding plants to distract their attention from the nest. Remove the largest chick from the nest, fit the ring and place the chick back in the nest, tucking the ringed chick well in. Hopefully, there will be no problems; if this is the case it is usually safe to ring the rest of the chicks the next day. If there are problems, the chicks will either need to be fostered out so they can be ringed or left with the parents as unringed and recorded as such. Many

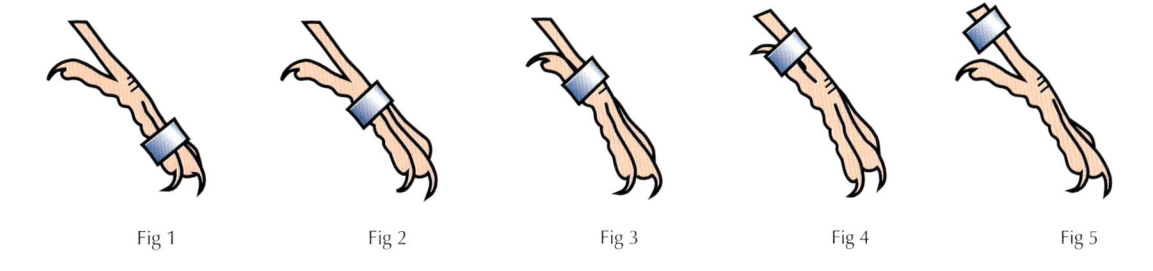

| Fig 1 | Fig 2 | Fig 3 | Fig 4 | Fig 5 |

Ringing young birds

breeders keep a few pairs of canaries who make good foster parents in such circumstances. If a hen has a bad attitude to rings it is unlikely she will change; on the other hand, if a hen accepts rings in the first place she can generally be relied upon with future nests of chicks.

The actual time of day chosen to ring chicks will depend on the breeder's own circumstances. Some breeders like to ring towards dusk in the belief that the hen will settle down on the ringed chicks. However, if she is going to reject them, she will undoubtedly do so when cleaning the nest the following morning. For this reason, some breeders like to ring in the early morning so that a watch can be kept on the hen. If she rejects, the chicks can be picked up before they expire and either put back with their rings removed or fostered out. If a hen accepts her chicks being ringed, it really makes little difference what time of day you ring them.

For the inexperienced breeder, who will undoubtedly take some time to complete the ringing operation, it is best to leave one chick in the nest. The remainder can be removed and placed in a lined canary nest pan or something similar. Leaving one chick in the nest prevents the hen from being concerned if she returns before ringing is completed. Do not expect to ring chicks easily the first time that you try. It takes practice and

Chapter 10

experience to become proficient at the task. Many breeders find it necessary to ring the birds before they are seven days old, but they should be aware of the problems. It is well worth practising on canaries and budgerigars, who are much more tolerant of interference.

The recommended method for ringing is as follows (see illustrations on previous page):
- As you look at the rings you will see that they are tapered slightly (caused by stamping the number on them). Always place the big end on first.
- It is essential to get the three long toes straight and parallel to each other. If the toes are crossed the ring will not go on. Sometimes it takes several goes to get the ring in this position (fig 1) because the young bird continually tries to clench its toes.
- A gentle pressure and slight twisting motion will now take the ring up over the ball of the foot (figs 2 and 3).
- The ring is then slid up the shank of the leg until the hind claw is released (figs 4 and 5).

Do not try to rush the job; it requires care and patience.

Pastel brambling hen

Chapter 11

Exhibition

The most important rule if you are to be successful on the show bench is to ensure that your birds have access to water for regular bathing. Some birds are reluctant to bathe, but usually follow suit when they see or hear other birds doing so. If they will not, or do not have access to bathing facilities, they should be sprayed regularly. Many successful exhibitors spray their birds if necessary, but prefer a bird to bathe naturally; the majority will, if given the opportunity. When a bird bathes, it relaxes, allowing the water to penetrate the feather; when sprayed, it behaves as if it is trying to avoid the water, 'tightening up'. Birds soon accept spraying, however, and many look forward to and enjoy it. Without any doubt, rain water is best for their plumage. This is what wild birds use and they always carry a 'sheen' or gloss on the feather, obtained by bathing frequently.

A bird should get used to its show cage before it is exhibited. The best arrangement is to hang a show cage onto the stock cage so that the bird can go in and out of it at will, or an old show cage with the door removed can be fixed in a suitable place in the aviary so that the bird can get used to it. Titbits in the show cage will encourage birds to enter it. Once familiar with a show cage, they can be confined in it for short periods. Make sure that they have water and learn to drink from the show cage drinker before they are exhibited. Bullfinches generally are not difficult to train and soon settle down and show themselves to advantage.

Young chaffinches and bramblings intended for exhibition can be housed as suggested in chapter 9: one or two to a roomy cage until they have completed their moult. If they have been housed in aviaries until they have finished their moult, they should be transferred to clean, good-sized stock cages, so that they can be steadied. After a few days, when the birds have settled down, they can be run into show cages for short periods. A little more patience will be needed with these birds than with those which have been cage moulted.

Some birds take to a show cage 'like a duck to water' as the saying goes, but others do not like to be confined. Such birds should be run into show cages for very short periods initially; eventually they will get accustomed to them. Occasionally one does meet a problem bird, but it is surprising how it will accept a show cage in time. Very often a bird, when shown at a small show for a few hours, gains con-

Chapter 11

Canary x bullfinch mule (mealy)

Exhibition

fidence. Once acquired, it is never lost. Frequent training so that the bird is used to the show cage and is quite comfortable in its surroundings is essential if the bird is to perform well at a show. It must stand well and move with confidence.

Some birds - just a few - have a nasty habit of facing the back of the cage. Such birds seldom overcome the habit. The ideal exhibition bird always faces the front of the cage. Any bird that proves difficult will need patience. Never push a bird so hard that you destroy its confidence. A few will never be steady enough for showing and these are best kept purely for breeding purposes.

When dealing with current-year birds, you should limit their training to short periods at first, returning them immediately after each session to their normal living quarters. Young birds are much more vulnerable to stress than adults, and losses will be experienced if they are put under too much stress too early in their lives. Never be in too much of a hurry to steady down that promising youngster. Patience is the key if you want to avoid disappointments.

The staging or presentation of British seedeaters, mules and hybrids is very important if the exhibitor is to be successful. There is a slight difference in the sizes of show cages advocated by the Scottish British Bird and Mule Club, but we are all agreed that green is the acceptable colour for interiors and black for exteriors. It is very important that exhibits are staged in the sizes advocated for the particular species. It is always permissible to use a larger cage but never a smaller one. Please remember that the sizes recommended and adopted are the minimum sizes and, in the main, the most suitable.

It is most important that show cages are made by skilled cage makers who specialise in this particular job. It is also very important that internal and external decoration of the show cage is of the highest standard. Sometimes we see show cages that are poorly constructed and decorated. A good bird deserves a good cage; it certainly enhances a bird's chances on the show bench.

Elderberry

To maintain show cages in good condition it is important that you always clean them after a show; wash them thoroughly, particularly the perches, and place them in your carrying case ready for your next show. They also need repainting periodically. If a little polish is put on the cage prior to the show, cleaning with warm water is easy afterwards.

It must be pointed out to those just beginning to exhibit birds that they are only allowed to be kept in show cages for 72 hours and while being transported to and from the shows. Also, it is only permissible to confine a bird in a show cage for training for a maximum of one hour in any 24. At other times, the birds must be kept in their aviaries or in the recommended stock cages.

Chapter 11

Cinnamon chaffinch cock

Exhibition

Show Cage
The correct show cage for the bullfinch, chaffinch and brambling and their various mules and hybrids is No 3:

	Length	Height	Depth
English Pattern	30.5cm (12in)	25.5cm (10in)	12.75cm (5in)
Scottish Pattern	28cm (11in)	25.5cm (10in)	12.75cm (5in)

Gauge wires: No 14, set at 2cm (0.75in) centres.
Drinking hole: 3cm (0.125in) diameter
Bottom rail: 3.75cm (1.5in) high
Top rail: (shaped) 2.5cm (1in) at the outside, sloping to 1.25cm (0.5in) at the centre.
Painted: Brolac Georgian Green inside and on the outside of the wires and on both top and bottom rails. The drinker should be painted the same green or made of green plastic. Black outside top, bottom, back and sides.

Groundsel

Exhibition Standard - Bullfinch
The exhibition bullfinch is cobby and round with a broad, expansive black cap extending well back over the head with clean-cut edges. The wings and tail are short and compact. The body colour is very important. The cock should have a light slate-blue back with bright even crimson starting from the throat down the chest, flanks, belly and between the legs, and a nicely-defined wing bar. Its rump is white and it has glossy black wings and tail. In the hen the back is richly suffused with brown and a rich chocolate brown replaces the crimson areas of the cock.

Size: As large as possible. 10 points
Type: Broad, full, well-rounded head with good rise. Set on full neck and well-rounded, short, thick-set body of strong, upstanding appearance. 30 points
Colour and Markings: Broad, clean-cut glossy black cap extending to back of skull. Well-defined clean-cut facial bib. Light, even slate-blue back. Glossy black wings and tail with well-defined pale slate wing bars. Bright, rich, even crimson colour throughout body extending well down between the legs to a clear white vent and rump. Hen's back is suffused, even brown with rich, even chocolate body colour. 30 points
Feather Quality and Condition: 15 points
Steadiness and Presentation: 15 points
Total: 100 points
Faults: Flat head, narrow cap, long-bodied, pale or impure colour, wing bars too light in colour, eye defects, deformities, poor presentation, insufficiently trained.
Notes: Yellow and buffs very evident. Buffs, though of less intensive colour, shall be given due consideration.

51

Chapter 11

Exhibition Standard - Chaffinch

A good exhibition chaffinch should be as large as possible with a good, upright stance, of reasonable length but full-bodied with a good full head to match. Cocks must have a rich even deep plum body colour. Hens should be rich grey with a tendency to slight pinkish fusion on the breast. In both sexes the shoulder and wing markings must be clear and distinct, though more defined in cocks. The standard is as follows:

Size: Large as possible. 15 points

Type: Full head, well cushioned at front, well filled bold-fronted body of strong appearance. 20 points

Colour and Markings: Head slate-blue with brownish overlay, chestnut back, olive-green rump, rich even plum-coloured chest, carried well down the body and between the legs to a whitish vent. Displaying good wing markings. Hens are olive-grey above and even rich grey below. 25 points.

Feather Quality and Condition: 10 points

Steadiness and Presentation: 30 points

Total: 100 points

Notes: Tendency for cocks to be larger than hens, buffs of less intensive colour.

Faults: Uneven or poor run of colour, lightness at throat, eye defects, deformities, poor presentation, insufficiently trained.

Exhibition Standard - Brambling

In an exhibition brambling colour and markings are of prime importance. Fuller-bodied and bolder than the chaffinch with deep rust-coloured waistcoat coming well down the breast and with a good run of colour into the flanks. The flank markings must be as profuse as possible and the spangling on the back even and distinct. Hens are less colourful, lacking the dark head and with less distinct back spangling, but must have good profuse flank markings. The standard is as follows:

Size: As large as possible. 15 points.

Type: Full head, well-cushioned at front, well-filled bold-fronted body of strong appearance. 10 points

Colour and Markings: Head black flecked with brown, plentiful, even spangling on back and flanks, rich, even rust-brown chest apron extending well down breast and into flanks. Hens are lighter shades of brown and must have profuse spangling, particularly on flanks, and lack black-hooded head of cock. 35 points.

Feather Quality and Condition: 10 points

Steadiness and Presentation: 30 points

Total: 100 points

Notes: Tendency for cocks to be larger than hens, buffs of less intensive colour.

Faults: Poor or uneven spangling, poor run of colour or break in apron, lightness at throat or around eyes (spectacles), poorly-defined hood or black in throat.

Beech

Chapter 12

Mules and hybrids

Mule is the fancier's term for offspring raised from a canary and a British finch; offspring from two British finches of different species are referred to as hybrids. Both types are really hybrids, and some show schedules refer to mules as canary hybrids. Mules and hybrids are bred for exhibition, song or ornamental purposes and are generally considered to be infertile. However, modern knowledge and the production of the red canary from the red-hooded siskin of South America suggest that some mules may be fertile when paired back to canaries, but perhaps not until they are two or three years old.

Good exhibition mules are produced from Norwich type canaries and sometimes from cross-breeds. The Norwich x Yorkshire cross has been used, and birds of a long-barrel type are preferred by some breeders. Best quality mules are generally obtained from jonque hens, either clear or lightly marked.

Bullfinches

Mules: Mules bred from a canary cock and a bullfinch hen are lovely birds - not easy to produce but no longer the rarities they once were. So far, there is no authenticated record of any young being bred from a bullfinch cock and a canary hen. In fact, there are no authenticated records of the cock bullfinch having sired anything other than a bullfinch. Why this should be is not known. What can be said is that it is not for the want of trying.

Any variety of domestic canary cock can be used to produce bullfinch mules, but good exhibition mules are usually produced from Norwich type canaries, generally from jonque (yellow) birds. Some breeders prefer to use clear or lightly-variegated cocks in the belief that they produce purer coloured mules, but dark and heavily-variegated yellow cocks have also produced some outstanding birds.

In the unlikely event of a proven pair becoming available they should be kept together more or less permanently. Should just one of a proven pair become available it should be paired with a new, unflighted partner. However, we will usually need to start from scratch. Select a vigorous, unflighted canary cock and a steady, unflighted hen bullfinch. They should be kept together in a large cage or small flight. Introduction should be as soon as possible after a successful moult so that they are together throughout the winter, giving

Chapter 12

Greenfinch x chaffinch hybrid cock

them plenty of time to get to know each other. Bullfinch hens can be a little tempestuous to start with but usually settle down. Do not expect success to come easily.

Bullfinch mules and hybrids are among the most beautiful and sought after. Many failures will usually precede success. When eggs are successfully hatched and young are reared, weaned and self-supporting, they

Mules and hybrids

should be removed to a large cage. In addition to dry seeds they should be provided with plenty of egg food and water together with soaked seed and greenfood. Add a little Caraphyll Red* to their water and egg food when they are about six weeks old, gradually increasing the amount to the required strength by about the 10-week stage to obtain good colour for exhibition. The jonque young are the most sought after, but a mealy is still a grand bird to possess.

Hybrids: Hybrid pairs generally need more space than muling pairs and are best housed in small flights or aviaries; otherwise the basic principles are the same as for muling. The bullfinch hen has produced hybrids with goldfinch, linnet, greenfinch and redpoll cocks, in that order of ease and regularity. Hybrids with siskin, twite and crossbill cocks have not been reared to maturity as yet in the United Kingdom but it is understood that they have been recorded at least once in mainland Europe so are well worth trying.

* Registered trade mark of Roche Products Ltd

Chaffinches and Bramblings

Chaffinch and brambling hybrids produced to date are few indeed, for which there could be a number of contributory factors. Perhaps they have not been tried enough. Since they are almost entirely insectivorous when rearing young there is no doubt their successful production requires a little more dedication in supplying their needs. They also require more space when breeding than many other hybrid pairs if some success is to be achieved. There is also the point that hens of both these species tend to be single brooded which considerably narrows down the chances of a hybrid being produced.

Chaffinch and brambling cocks have failed to produce with any species other than than each other, where they are highly fertile: Chaffinch x Brambling and Brambling x Chaffinch have been produced on numerous occasions. Unfortunately from an exhibition point of view, they seem to favour their brambling parent in rather more than a 50:50 proportion. Good specimens that clearly show both sides of their parentage can do very well on the show bench, even in the keenest of competition.

All other chaffinch and brambling hybrids produced to date have involved hens of the named species. Chaffinch and brambling hens are usually excellent parents, so foster parents are rarely needed. To produce and successfully rear hybrids from these birds you will usually have to house them in flights or aviaries. The intended hybridising pair should be introduced to each other as soon as possible so that they can familiarise and hopefully bond.

Although chaffinch and brambling cocks are noted for their aggression during the breeding period, hens of the species are usually no trouble at all, and a hen of either species can safely be housed in a mixed aviary of reasonable size. Success is more likely where the hybrid pair have a flight or aviary to themselves and where there is competition neither for nesting sites nor, more importantly, for the live food needed to rear the young. The rearing, weaning, housing, moulting and training is as advised for the species. All hybrids intended for exhibition will need to be colour fed.

As far as chaffinch hybrids are concerned, Greenfinch x Chaffinch is the most frequently produced, and

Plantain

Chapter 12

a good one will do extremely well on the show bench. Other hybrids produced from chaffinch hens are Goldfinch x Chaffinch and Redpoll x Chaffinch. To our knowledge there has only been one authenticated record of a Canary x Chaffinch mule bred in the United Kingdom. This would be well worth trying, as would Siskin x Chaffinch, Linnet x Chaffinch, Twite x Chaffinch and Crossbill x Chaffinch.

Brambling hybrids are even rarer. To our knowledge, with the exception of Brambling x Chaffinch, the only records are of Greenfinch x Brambling and Redpoll x Brambling. Three of the former have been recorded but unfortunately all were hens. Only one of the latter has been produced to date so there is plenty of scope for someone seeking a challenge in hybrid production. Others worth trying are the Canary x Brambling mule and the hybrids Goldfinch x Brambling, Siskin x Brambling, Linnet x Brambling, Twite x Brambling and Crossbill x Brambling.

Greenfinch x bullfinch hybrid cock

Chapter 13

Mutations and Colour Variants

It is not the intention of this book to delve too deeply into the world of genetics. However, some basic understanding of the genetic inheritance patterns of colour mutations is necessary if we are to control, improve and generally make the best use of these mutations.

There are three modes of inheritance: dominant, recessive sex-linked and recessive autosomal. If we were to look deeper within each of these groups we would find deviations such as incomplete dominants and full dominants, multiple alleles and deep recessives. If you wish to delve further into the subject you will find that many books have been published about it.

MUTATION INHERITANCE CHARTS

The following charts are for the guidance of those taking up the breeding of colour variants and can be applied to any species. However, they refer only to pairings involving the use of a single mutated colour form with that of pure normal, not to cross-colour pairing expeditions. The latter involve more than one colour form and are covered elsewhere.

Note

In the charts and pairing expectations used throughout, the cock is always listed first in the pairings and the following symbols are used:

/ denotes 'split', carrier of the mutation.

- when between two varieties, refers to a composite variety.

SF denotes single-factor dominant, and

DF denotes double-factor dominant

= denotes progeny expectations.

Recessive, Sex-linked Mutation Chart
(referred to as **Sex-linked**)

Normal/Sex-linked	x	Normal	=	Normal Cocks, Normal/Sex-linked Cocks, Normal Hens, Sex-linked Hens
Normal	x	Sex-linked	=	Normal/Sex-linked Cocks, Normal Hens
Normal/sex-linked	x	Sex-linked	=	Normal/Sex-linked Cocks, Sex-linked Cocks, Normal Hens, Sex-linked Hens
Sex-linked	x	Normal	=	Normal/Sex-linked Cocks, Sex-linked Hens
Sex-linked	x	Sex-linked	=	Sex-linked Cocks, Sex-linked Hens

Recessive Autosomal Mutation Chart
(referred to as **Recessive**)

Normal/Recessive	x	Normal	=	Normal Cocks, Normal/Recessive Cocks, Normal Hens, Normal/Recessive Hens
(Reverse Pairing gives same expectations)				
Normal/Recessive	x	Normal/Recessive	=	Normal Cocks, Normal/Recessive Cocks, Recessive Cocks, Normal Hens, Normal/Recessive Hens, Recessive Hens
Recessive	x	Normal	=	Normal/Recessive Cocks, Normal/Recessive Hens
(Reverse Pairing gives same expectations)				
Recessive	x	Normal/Recessive	=	Normal/Recessive Cocks, Recessive Cocks, Normal/Recessive Hens, Recessive Hens
(Reverse Pairing gives same expectations)				
Recessive	x	Recessive	=	Recessive Cocks, Recessive Hens

Dominant Mutation Chart

Dominant (SF)	x	Normal	=	Normal Cocks, Dominant (SF) Cocks, Normal Hens, Dominant (SF) Hens
(Reverse Pairing gives same expectations)				
Dominant (SF)	x	Dominant (SF)	=	Normal Cocks, Dominant (SF) Cocks, Dominant (DF) Cocks, Normal Hens, Dominant (SF) Hens, Dominant (DF) Hens
Dominant (SF)	x	Dominant (DF)	=	Dominant (SF) Cocks, Dominant (DF) Cocks, Dominant (SF) Hens, Dominant (DF) Hens
(Reverse Pairing gives same expectations)				
Dominant (DF)	x	Normal	=	Dominant (SF) Cocks, Dominant (SF) Hens
(Reverse Pairing gives same expectations)				
Dominant (DF)	x	Dominant (DF)	=	Dominant (DF) Cocks, Dominant (DF) Hens

SPONTANEOUS SPORTS

Mutated colour forms appear from time to time through spontaneous sports and, unless these are preserved by correct matings, they can disappear as quickly as they came. Some understanding of genetics will certainly increase our ability to perpetuate mutations through these chance arrivals by enabling us to discover the mode of inheritance. This is secondary to establishing the colour form and follows through from the elimination of inheritance modes one at a time.

Mutations and Colour Variants

Opal chaffinch cock

Chapter 13

Dominant Mutations

These are the easiest to establish, since a visual colour form of this mutation is capable of producing its own likeness in the first generation, irrespective of its sex and without any inbreeding.

When you are breeding dominants the colour form is visual and cannot be carried by a normal in hidden form (generally known as a split form). New colour forms that are dominant mutations can turn up as spontaneous sports at any time, male or female, but they are always in what is known as 'single-factor' form, an incomplete dominant. As will be seen from the chart, when one of these is paired to a normal, half of the progeny are of the mutation colour. However, when two single factors of the mutation are paired together they produce young of which 25% are of normal colour and 75% of the mutated colour. Of the mutated young, 25% will receive a double dose of the factor producing the mutation (known as 'double-factor') and they may be visually different (in a dilute factor, much paler) or appear the same. Double-factor forms of the mutation are fully dominant and, when paired to normals, produce all mutation young of the single-factor type. So it will be seen that dominant mutations are not only the easiest to establish but also lend themselves to improvements in exhibition qualities when paired to good exhibition-type normals.

Spearthistle

Recessive Sex-linked Mutations

These are not so easy to establish. Although the rules governing sex-linked inheritance are quite straightforward it is important to remember that the results from pairing a sex-linked cock of a mutated colour form to a normal hen are quite different to those obtained from pairing a normal-coloured cock to a sex-linked mutation hen. The reason for this is that a cock can be either pure normal or a visual normal bird with the ability to pass on the colour mutation to some of his young (referred to as a 'carrier' or 'split') or of a visual mutated colour form; whereas a hen can only be a normal-coloured bird or a visual colour mutation. In other words, a normal-coloured hen cannot be split for the sex-linked mutation; she is what you see. Unfortunately there is no significant visual difference between a normal cock and a visual normal cock carrying the mutation factor, so its true genetic make-up can only be proven through test matings. However, as can be seen from the chart, certain matings produce visual normal cocks guaranteed to be carriers of the mutation.

When a sex-linked colour mutation turns up, the first bird of the mutated form is always a hen. If such a hen is paired to a normal-colour cock all the young produced, both cocks and

Shepherd's Purse

hens, will be of normal colour, but all the young cocks, although of normal appearance, will carry the new colour. If these young cocks are paired to normal hens 25% of the young produced will be of the mutation colour. Because of the mode of inheritance these will all be hens, and normal hens will also be produced. All the young cocks produced will be visual normals, half of them pure normal and the other half carriers of the mutation colour. These young cocks would need to be test-mated to find out which are carrying the mutated gene.

It follows that, to establish the new colour in the shortest possible time, we need to obtain a new-colour cock. To do this we must resort to inbreeding, pairing a new-colour hen to either her father or one of her sons: a practice which should not be taken too far because it can lead to infertility, dead-in-shell or deformed and weak chicks. Once the new-colour cock has been produced it can be paired to an unrelated normal hen. All the young hens of the pairing will then be of the mutated colour and all the young cocks will be of normal appearance but carrying the mutation. These are called 'carriers' or 'splits' and shown as 'normal/mutation' on the tables. When sufficient distantly-related cocks and hens of the new colour are produced they can be paired together to give a clutch in which all the young, cocks and hens, are of the new mutated colour form.

Recessive Autosomal Mutations

Because of their mode of inheritance, these can be difficult to establish. Inbreeding is necessary at first to establish these colour forms, despite the hazards described above. It is important to remember that, unlike the dominants and sex-linked mutations, splits occur in both cocks and hens.

It is also important to realise that the mutation must be present in both parents before visual examples can be produced. Recessive mutations can be carried for many generations in hidden split form but, when two splits come together, the visual form of the mutation will be produced. These can be either cocks or hens. You can then pair these back to the opposite-sex parent. Such a pairing will produce more of the mutation in visual form and all the non-visual young produced will be carriers of the mutation.

This method will achieve results in the shortest possible time but, as already discussed, at the risk of producing weak and sickly mutation young. In the long term it would be better to outcross with the visual mutation by pairing it to one, two or more unrelated normals. This pairing, although not producing any visual forms of the mutation, would produce all young splits for the mutation. You can then pair these more distantly related birds together, split x split, producing much stronger young of the mutated colour form and thus ensuring a better chance of the survival and establishment of the mutation.

BULLFINCH COLOUR VARIANTS

Reports of colour variants in this species have always been few and far between but over the years there have been some - mainly birds showing varying areas of white feathering, but also mutation forms. Dilute, pastel, cinnamon and at least two different forms of albinos have been bred: one in which all pigment is suppressed, giving a visually all-white bird, and another in which the melanin pigments are almost completely suppressed but the red pigment is only slightly reduced. The male of the latter mutation is an extremely beautiful bird. To date only two mutations of this species can be considered to be established, both in Europe and mainly by Belgian breeders. They are being bred in the United Kingdom but at present only have a tentative foothold. Both of these established colour forms are sex-linked in their inheritance patterns.

The first to be established was the pastel. The effect is an overall dilution and appears variable. The best coloured examples come from Pastel x Pastel matings though some good examples have also been produced from Normal/Pastel x Pastel matings.

The cinnamon was the second mutation to be established. It follows the conventional rules of sex-linked cinnamon reproduction and is another very attractive mutation. As both mutations are sex-linked in character

Chapter 13

we shall soon no doubt see the pastel form of the cinnamon being bred, as its production would be relatively simple:

Pastel × Cinnamon = Normal/Pastel/Cinnamon Cocks, Pastel Hens.

These double-split cocks can then be paired back to produce a cross-over. Irrespective of the colour of the hen used, a percentage of the cross-over pastel-cinnamons will be produced:

Normal/Pastel/Cinnamon × Normal = Normal Cocks, Normal/Pastel Cocks,
Normal/Cinnamon Cocks, Normal/Pastel/Cinnamon Cocks,
Normal Hens, Pastel Hens, Cinnamon Hens,
Pastel-Cinnamon Hens.

Normal/Pastel/Cinnamon × Pastel = Normal/Pastel Cocks, Normal/Pastel/Cinnamon Cocks,
Pastel Cocks, Pastel/Cinnamon Cocks, Normal Hens,
Pastel Hens, Cinnamon Hens, Pastel-Cinnamon Hens.

Normal/Pastel/Cinnamon × Cinnamon = Normal/Cinnamon Cocks, Normal/Pastel/Cinnamon Cocks,
Cinnamon Cocks, Cinnamon/Pastel Cocks, Normal Hens,
Cinnamon Hens, Pastel Hens, Pastel-Cinnamon Hens.

Unfortunately for breeders in the United Kingdom, both of these established mutations originated in the northern race of bullfinch, so it will take a number of years of dedicated breeding to transfer the mutations into our own native race before they are generally accepted within the British Bird Classes. Not an easy task but, given time, it will be achieved, as will the establishment of other mutations.

CHAFFINCH AND BRAMBLING COLOUR VARIANTS

Reports of colour variations among wild chaffinches, while not numerous, have been fairly constant over the years. Whites, pieds, cinnamons and various forms of dilute have all been recorded. Domestic-bred chaffinches have produced a number of colour mutations, most of which originated in continental Europe, where this species is very popular. It is especially popular in Belgium, where it is bred not only for general avicultural purposes but also for song contests. Established colour mutations are sex-linked silver (agate), sex-linked pastel and Isabel, recessive cinnamon (brown) and recessive silver (opal). Other colours such as sex-linked cinnamon, whites and pieds are being bred but not yet fully established. The small number of these colour mutations being bred by dedicated breeders in the United Kingdom only have a tentative foothold at present.

Larch

There have been reports of white, pied and dilute forms of brambling appearing in the wild but these have been few and far between; rather surprising considering that flocks numbering more than a million birds have been recorded for this species. Domestic-bred bramblings have produced colour variants in pied, cinnamon and pastel forms but at present none has been fully established.

Fortunately, present-day breeders are much more knowledgeable about the genetics involved in colour mutations and, given time, we are sure many more colour variants in chaffinches and bramblings will become fully established within aviculture.

Chapter 14

The Law

It is beyond the scope of this volume to give a full explanation of the Wild Life and Countryside Act 1981, which is the current bird protection act; it is both long and complicated. All keepers and breeders of birds, especially of our native British birds, should make themselves fully acquainted with its provisions. Copies of the act can be obtained from HM Stationary Office. However, some of the most important points are as follows:

1. All wild birds, their nests and eggs are protected.
2. It is illegal to have any wild bird in your possession unless you have a special licence or permit to do so. A bird is only considered to be legally captive bred if its parents were legally in captivity at the time that it was hatched in a cage or aviary. If you can prove that, the bird need not be ringed; but it is recommended that whenever possible all young birds are ringed.
3. It is illegal to buy or sell a native bird except by special licence unless it is listed only on Schedule 3 Part 1 of the Wild Life and Countryside Act 1981, and then again provided that it is correctly ringed with an approved ring of the correct size. The chaffinch and brambling are so listed, but the bullfinch is listed under Schedule 2 Part 2, so slightly different rules apply (see the section **Bullfinches as Pests** in chapter 3).
4. Except under special licence, only birds listed on Schedule 3 Part 1 can be exhibited, and again they must be ringed with an approved ring of the correct size.
5. It is illegal to keep or confine any bird whatsoever in a cage that is not sufficient in height, length or breadth to permit the bird to stretch its wings freely except when:
   (a) the bird is in the course of conveyance.
   (b) the bird is undergoing treatment by a veterinary surgeon.
   (c) the bird is being exhibited for competition. (However, it must not remain in a show cage for more than 72 hours.)
   (d) the bird is being trained for exhibition. (However, it must not be so confined for more than one hour in any 24-hour period.)

63

Bullfinches, Chaffinches & Bramblings

Tribute

Sadly Peter Lander died before the series *Popular British Birds in Aviculture* could be published.

I first met Peter in the early 1960s when he approached me for some Siberian goldfinches. The goldfinch was a species for which he had a particular fondness.

In addition to keeping and breeding birds, Peter had a keen interest in all things ornithological. I found him a quiet, unassuming man who knew his own mind. He was the driving force behind the founding of The British Bird Council, and worked tirelessly on its behalf for many years. In recent years, by his own choice, he took a back seat, but was always there when needed to give advice and a helping hand.

I worked with Peter when he compiled *British Birds in Aviculture* for the British Bird Council and felt privileged when he asked me to be co-author of the *Popular British Birds in Aviculture* series. Without Peter's initiative this series would not have been produced.

A guiding light extinguished, but memories will light our way.

Bob Partridge